Praise for *We Got This*

"Remember when adults asked your younger self, 'Who's your hero?' and you named your favorite president or pop star? After reading *We Got This*, I dare you not to revisit that question. The 75 diverse single mothers in this extraordinary collection have married their fierce love for their children with their fierce skills as writers. Their voices whisper and bellow, protest and rejoice, hum and sing. Collectively, they announce: single moms are our unsung heroes."

—Alma Gottlieb, coauthor of *A World of Babies:
Imagined Childcare Guides for Eight Societies*

"*We Got This* is fierce love meets fear meets wonder. I savored these poems and essays, which are full of humor and heartbreak, wisdom and humanity. These pieces will help any mother—single or not—to feel inspired and supported, seen and understood, as she navigates this tremendous thing called motherhood."

—Kate Hopper, author of *Ready for Air: A Journey Through
Premature Motherhood* and *Use Your Words:
A Writing Guide for Mothers*

"The voices in *We Got This* are touching, vulnerable, hilarious, insightful, bold, strong, resilient, and brilliant. Whether you are facing single motherhood, you are a single mom, or you love one, this book is a mirror to the special life experience of solo mothering—and solo thriving."

—Emma Johnson, founder, Wealthysinglemommy.com, and
author of *The Kickass Single Mom*

"*We Got This* is a reunion of survivors. No 'how-to' here, just a loving village of women who have been there, who are still there, and who reach out a hand to you, single mom, to help you get your bearings. Within these pages, you will find encouraging strength and the promise of finding your own joy."

—M. M. De Voe, founder, director, Pen Parentis, Ltd.

"Isolated, scared, sad, and hopeless are some of the emotions I felt when I was going through my divorce eleven years ago. I had two small children and no family living near me, and I had never felt so alone. I wish I could have read *We Got This* back then. Reading this book made me feel like I had friends, women who understand me, who care about me, and who are here for me, and like no matter what, everything is going to be OK!"
—Jackie Pilossoph, creator, Divorced Girl Smiling, and "Love Essentially" columnist for Chicago Tribune Media Group

"The collection of stories in *We Got This* is a beautifully crafted testament to the universe of solo motherhood that connects women who feel like strangers, in the most intimate of ways."
—Deborah Gruenfeld, professor and codirector, Executive Program in Women's Leadership, Stanford University

"*We Got This* is a terrific collection of voices of solo moms—and their kids. The laments and triumphs of these mothers filled me with awe and laughter, and made me proud to belong to the human race."
—Sari Wilson, author of *Girl Through Glass*

"*We Got This* brings hope, light, joy, and humor to the seemingly dark road of being a solo mom—a job that we often don't choose and that we can't quit. The stories shared in this collection brought me great joy because they are heartfelt depictions of the solo mom reality. Go get yourself a copy. You will be glad you did."
—Noelle Federico, business consultant and founder, Theworkingsinglemom.com

We Got This

SOLO MOM STORIES OF
GRIT, HEART, AND HUMOR

Edited by Marika Lindholm, Cheryl Dumesnil,
Domenica Ruta, and Katherine Shonk

SHE WRITES PRESS

Published 2019
Printed in the United States of America
ISBN: 978-1-63152-656-5 pbk
ISBN: 978-1-63152-657-2 ebk
Library of Congress Control Number: 2019939483

For information, address:
She Writes Press
1569 Solano Ave #546
Berkeley, CA 94707

She Writes Press is a division of SparkPoint Studio, LLC.

Interior design by Tabitha Lahr

All company and/or product names may be trade names, logos, trademarks, and/or registered trademarks and are the property of their respective owners.

Names and identifying characteristics have been changed to protect the privacy of certain individuals.

Editors' note: Throughout, capitalization of races/ethnicities reflects authors' personal preferences.

Contents

Introduction.. xiii
Marika Lindholm

CHAPTER ONE: THE KIDS ARE ALRIGHT

The Road 3
Teresa Mei Chuc

You Were Born to Be Loved................................ 4
Domenica Ruta

from *The Light of the World: A Memoir* 8
Elizabeth Alexander

When One Door Closes, Another One Opens 12
Terri Linton

Notes to My Autistic Daughter 15
Marianne Peel Forman

I Was the Different One 18
Nisa Rashid

Return... 24
Dorianne Laux

Teaching My Son to Write: An Abecedarian 26
Stacia Fleegal

It's Really Not a Big Deal 28
Jacob Kronenberg

An Open Letter to Our Sperm Donor 31
Robin Silbergleid

Dad Day: Death Is a Holiday 33
Lennlee Keep

How to Pray 38
Sage Cohen

Butterfly and Sunshine 40
Marika Lindholm

CHAPTER TWO: LEAN ON ME

Finding My Voice, Feeding My Friends 49
Janelle Hardy

For My Sisters 53
Sharisse Kimbro

from *A Beautiful, Terrible Thing* 57
Jen Waite

Raising a Boy without a Man 64
Kathleen Laccinole

September 17 69
Anne Lamott

Prayer 72
Keetje Kuipers

The Godfather 74
Margot Kessler

the lost women 77
Lucille Clifton

We Are Loved 78
Amy Rivers

XIII 82
Adrienne Rich

Tahlequah 83
Isa Down

All the Single Ladies 84
Jennifer Baumgardner

CHAPTER THREE: A DAY IN THE LIFE

When a Car Wreck Collides with Picking Up the Kids 93
Melissa Stephenson

How to Comfort a Small Child 96
Abby Murray

Rules for Being Twenty 99
Ariel Gore

Evening Guilt 102
Kristie Robin Johnson

I'm the Woman Who Hit Your Daughter with My Car 105
Courtney Christine

Life after the NICU 112
Sarah Netter

My Life as a Refugee 116
Faleeha Hassan

The Rookie 121
January Gill O'Neil

This Is Your Life 123
Fern Capella

Crying It Out 128
Robin Silbergleid

They Give Awards for That 130
Lee Nash

CHAPTER FOUR: GOOD MORNING HEARTACHE

Why We Stay 135
VersAnnette Blackman-Bosia

When He Died 138
Robin Rogers

This Lesson I Know My Boy Already Knows 142
Georgia Pearle

from *The Light of the World: A Memoir* 144
Elizabeth Alexander

Then 148
Ruth Stone

When Black Lives Matter More Than You Ever Imagined 150
Deborah Oster Pannell

In a Quiet Moment 154
Hilary Melton

Heroin, Rain 156
Anne Spollen

On Home 161
Lisa Fay Coutley

What I Will Tell His Daughter, When She's
Old Enough to Ask 163
Meg Day

Grey Street 165
Angela Ricketts

CHAPTER FIVE: A CHANGE IS GONNA COME

Now That I Am Forever with Child 173
Audre Lorde

Coming Out Pregnant! 175
Staceyann Chin

The Story, for Now 181
Janlori Goldman

Myths of Botany and Motherhood 185
Isa Down

Gravity 189
Kim Addonizio

The Nervous Hospital. 190
Mary Karr

What Remains. 195
Jaimie Seaton

It Will Look Like a Sunset 200
Kelly Sundberg

Cicadas 213
Rachel Jamison Webster

My Books on Divorce 215
Amy Poehler

Today, I Am Mostly Crying 221
Claire Gillespie

CHAPTER SIX: ISN'T IT ROMANTIC?

Size Queen 227
Evie Peck

All Manner of Obscene Things 232
Kim Addonizio

Origami Wishes. 234
Akesha Baron

How My Daughter Taught Me to Trust Again. 238
Rachel Sarah

Personals 242
Muriel Johnson

Kaboom 243
Susan Goldberg

I Don't Want Your Husband 250
P. Charlotte Lindsay

How to Love. 253
January Gill O'Neil

You Can't "Undo" This One. 255
Jessica Bern

I Ask the Impossible 259
Ana Castillo

CHAPTER SEVEN: HERE COMES THE SUN

Yeah, But 263
Cheryl Dumesnil

My Birth, My Way. 270
Cate Morrissey

How I Came to Me 273
Malaika King Albrecht

Teacher and Teammate 276
Sarah Kowalski

The Sky Is Everywhere. 282
Nancy Sharp

Divorce Cliché. 284
Shannon Lell

Sunday. 287
January Gill O'Neil

Why I Don't Grieve for My Daughter at College 289
Ylonda Gault

Deconstructing Kanji 293
Mika Yamamoto

After He Left 297
Jeanie Tomasko

I'd Loved Before, but Never Like This. 300
asha bandele

Contributors 303

Permissions and Acknowledgments. .325

Introduction

Hey Mama,

Almost two decades ago, when my children were three and five, I went through a painful and difficult divorce. As a sociologist specializing in gender issues, I thought I had a handle on the challenges ahead. Not so! During my first year as a solo mom, I was often sick, stressed, and lonely. Like most moms who go through a divorce, I felt tremendous guilt, my finances suffered, and friends who were uncomfortable with my new identity drifted away. Our family of three ultimately found joy in our small apartment, where I slept on the couch, but those early years of solo motherhood convinced me that single mothers unequivocally need more support, more empathy, and more praise. That's why in 2015, I founded Empowering Solo Moms Everywhere (ESME) to build a helpful and informative community for single moms (who, in America alone, are currently raising fifteen million children). Inspired by ESME, *We Got This: Solo Mom Stories of Grit, Heart, and Humor* is a love letter from our community of solo moms who want you to know that you are not alone. Your tenacity, resilience, and grit are worthy of celebration.

Too often, single mothers are voiceless or misrepresented in a sea of stereotypes, accusations, and shame. My coeditors—Cheryl, Domenica, and Katie—and I take great pride in sharing poems, essays, and quotes that reflect the diversity of single motherhood while affirming the collective challenges and rewards of parenting alone. The stories in *We Got This* come from divorced moms, widows, military moms, single moms by choice, and single moms by surprise. They come from moms of all ages raising kids of all ages. Our authors represent a range of ethnicities, economic circumstances, sexual orientations, and beliefs. The chapters in *We Got This* blend humor, gravitas, pride, and hope as they progress through the many themes of solo motherhood: "The Kids Are Alright" (raising children), "Lean on Me" (finding support), "A Day in the Life" (everyday challenges), "Good Morning Heartache" (a difficult shift in identity), "A Change Is Gonna Come" (growth and resilience), "Isn't It Romantic?" (dating), and "Here Comes the Sun" (hope and optimism). *We Got This* amplifies the voices of single moms in all our gorgeous variations, celebrating who we are and what we do.

Like the songs that inspire each chapter, the solo mom stories we've selected resonate through honesty and revelation. From a military spouse suffering a heart attack while her husband is deployed to a mom who "lost" her spouse to mental illness, these voices draw us in with confidence and grace. Written by authors ranging from well-known to yet-to-be-discovered, these poems and essays are beautifully crafted and speak to both the head and the heart. The array of feelings these writers express—yearning, melancholy, hope, strength, shame, regret, fear, ferocity, bravery, rebellion, anticipation, longing, rapture, and triumph—remind us that a solo mom's journey is, by necessity, contradictory. Society undervalues us and offers paltry support, yet due to fierce love for our children, we display bravery and strength again and again.

We hope, after you read the stories in *We Got This*, that you feel like you've just had a conversation with a group of friends who get it—the kind of friends who recognize your strength and mirror it back to you. By the end of the book, we want readers to see that, as we say at ESME, "Solo doesn't mean alone." We are part of a community of resilient women who, despite hardship and some pain, can thrive and find joy as solo moms. We dedicate this book to all of you who love unconditionally, always show up, find humor in difficult situations, get back up after you fall, defy the odds, and accomplish the impossible, day after day, year after year.

We see you. We hear you. And we know you got this!

Much love,
Marika

Chapter One:
The Kids Are Alright

My brother and I grew up in the projects. But through my mother's emphasis on education, we are living wonderful, full lives, liberated from the shackles of poverty.

—Supreme Court Justice Sonia Sotomayor

The Road

Teresa Mei Chuc

I say my children are
like lightning bugs.

I see how they
glow in the dark.

Sometimes, it is
the only light I see.

You Were Born to Be Loved

Domenica Ruta

It is a Sunday morning gleaming with possibility, and I don't want to leave our apartment. You are staring out the window at the chiseled skyline of Manhattan, the Empire State Building a tiny spear poking up in the center, the elevated track of the subway rushing past every seven minutes, to your endless delight. The sun is gaping, ready, invincible. I have never been more tired.

There should be a new word for solo mom exhaustion. It's an accumulated sleep deficit that warps the mind beyond recognition. Only medical students, soldiers, and certain drug addicts could compare notes. For the first few months you were here, so tiny and wrinkled, nothing but eyes and hair more closely resembling fur, day and night became indistinguishable to me, and I did not close my eyes long enough to have dreams. I got little sips of sleep: forty-five minutes here, then up again to feed you, another hour there, if I was lucky; naps, really, all of them too short to check into that hotel of magic where all the garbage of the mind, the fear and anxiety, is sorted into compost.

But every so-called morning, I got up with a surge of love and adrenaline. We had days I don't remember now, but pray I will see again in the moments before I die. Because they were wonderful. You were wonderful. And so I get up this morning, too, like all the others, to play with you.

Mornings with my own solo mom were very different when I was a child. My mother was almost always too hungover to get up and play with me—to get up at all. I don't remember those mornings well, either—only the bleary mood they evoke. Like the exhaustion I feel now, there is no singular word that can accurately define it: a strange intersection of loneliness and physical hunger, longing, and fear, a feeling as real as a punch in the stomach and the emptiness that follows it. Those childhood mornings, a realm of solitude lived alongside a sleeping body, my mother unwakeable as a corpse, sent me deep into my imagination for entertainment and consolation, for better and for worse. I climbed the cabinets in search of food when I was a toddler no bigger than you. There was no telling when she would wake to feed me. Even when she did finally get up sometime in the afternoon, awake but not, there was no guarantee she would stay very long. The urge to get high again pulled her away from me.

Looking at us now—you, needing a good hair brushing and a bath; me, unwilling to take you anywhere that requires me to wear a bra—I wonder, are we so much better off? But this is ridiculous, a slip into self-loathing greased by exhaustion. Because *of course we are!* My mother was a hardened drug addict, and I am several years clean and sober. I got sober for my own good, years before you were a possibility. Now I stay sober for us both, one day at a time. After you got all your shots, I'd take you to the church basements where the alcoholics meet. Everyone would fight over who got to hold you next, while my shoulders ached in that brief moment of weightlessness.

But this weekend is my weekend with you, an alternating bimonthly holiday I put too much pressure on. I should take you to the zoo. I should take a shower. I should be giving you a more enriching experience of this Sunday. I'm so, so tired.

You have taken every single toy off your shelves and scattered them across the apartment. Our kitchen floor is a sprawling miniature parking lot of racecars and bulldozers. You're getting cranky, on the verge of a nap—something you so desperately need, even more than I do—but you're fighting it, like you always do. To make you laugh, I find the wooden animals of your two different jungle-themed puzzles and stand them up in a little menagerie. I make introductions, like at a dinner party, with the giraffe from one puzzle greeting the giraffe from the other puzzle.

"*Bonjour*," the goofier-looking lion says to his compatriot.

"Hello," the small-eyed lion replies.

"Oh, *mais oui. Je suis désolé*. I thought you spoke French. Your country was not colonized by the Belgians?"

"The British," the other lion says, rather stiffly.

"*Mais oui*," the goofy lion says again, because my imaginary French is limited.

"May whee!" you repeat joyously. "May wheeeeee!"

Of the two elephants in the puzzles, one is clearly a baby. He trots up close to the elder elephant and asks, "What are those called?"

"Tusks," the big elephant explains. She is more cartoonish, her colors more garish. I wonder if her backstory involves a stint in the circus. "You'll have them too one day."

"Oh," says the grave little elephant. "All the grown-ups in my pack were slaughtered, so I don't know about tusks."

"Don't worry. I'll teach you."

The hippos are in your control, so they just make a lot of fart noises.

On the computer, Lou Reed's "Walk on the Wild Side" is playing, as per your screeching demand, on repeat. A cloud of dread amasses in my chest when the "colored girls go do-do-do-do-do . . ." One day I will have to explain to you why he called them "colored girls." You don't yet know that I am white and you are brown and what that means, above all else, is that you are not safe. You'll learn about the vile things that happened to your ancestors and the wretched things that continue to happen to people like you. Your history on both sides is gouged by tragedy: racism and poverty, your father's family inheritance from colonialism; addiction, violence, and rape, my family's legacy of self-perpetuating trauma. There are so many things you are going to learn, things beyond my control: heroin and the N-word and murder and suicide and injustice and disease and good old-fashioned heartache. No wonder I don't want to take you outside.

I skip to a Lucinda Williams song, "You Were Born to Be Loved," and you begin to rub your eyes. The nap is getting closer. I never had bedtimes as a child; there was no routine, no person, to see me off to sleep. I would pass out in the clothes I had on that day, sometimes on the floor, at whatever time my eyes dropped shut, and wake up to figure it all out again by myself. But not you, not us. I rock you in my arms, and you smile a coy smile, because you know exactly what I'm about to say.

"Remember when you were a baby, and you couldn't walk or talk or even hold up your head, and I had to hold you in my arms like this all the time?"

It's our tradition for me to repeat these words every time I hold you like this, to pretend you are such a big kid now, so different from that baby you were a blink ago.

I wish I could remember that time more. The details were so piercing in the moment; the whole of existence seemed to smolder between your long eyelashes. What I remember most is being so in love and so lonely at the same time, so afraid and so happy. And, that you hated to sleep, as you do now, and so I just held you all the time, because I didn't know what else to do.

"Again," you say softly of the song playing now. You have found a new lullaby. I lay down in your bed, still holding you, and together we drift off to sleep. We dream.

from *The Light of the World: A Memoir*

Elizabeth Alexander

The day he died, the four of us were exactly the same height, just over five foot nine. We'd measured the boys in the pantry doorway the week before. It seemed a perfect symmetry, a whole family the same size but in different shapes. Now the children grow past me and past their father. They seem to grow by the day; they sprout like beanstalks towards the sky.

Week after week I continue to watch them at basketball practice with our beloved Coach Geraldine. I listen to how they deepen their voices to holler, "Ball!" Coach G. tells Solo, "Get large!" or, as his father told him, "Never be smaller than you are." Be large. I watch how the young men on the team intimidate each other on purpose, how they enact their masculinity, in each other's faces, with controlled aggression that sometimes bursts over, and how they manage the aggression. I watch them knock each other down and help each other up. I watch them master the codes of the court and the street. I watch them practice their swag. They are smelling themselves, as the expression goes, literally smelling their funk, feeling the possibility of their maleness. I watch their splendiferous gloating when they make a three-pointer, how they yell, "Beast!" to each other when they snatch a rebound. And I watch how they give each other skin for each job well done, this fellowship of beautiful young men, learning to be mighty together inside of this gym with an inspirational woman coach who loves them and is showing them how to be large, skilled, savvy young men living fully in their physicality after their father's body so suddenly stopped working.

Simon's ankle bones appear shiny at his pants' hems. He complains his feet hurt, and, indeed, his toes have grown and are pushing against the ends of his shoes. His growing seems avid, fevered. It feels like the insistent force of life itself. Ficre looked forward to seeing his sons grow beyond him. If I could hear him, I would hear him laughing his great laugh at this latest development.

I go to sleep with them on my mind, I wake up with them on my mind, and all my decisions are informed by their presence in my life. I think that's what all moms do.

—Sheryl Crow

When One Door Closes, Another One Opens

Terri Linton

My earliest memory of my father is not of us walking through a park, going for ice cream, or of me, with legs dangling, surveying the world atop his shoulders. Instead, it's of me waiting—for him. I'm dressed in a wool coat that's buttoned all the way up to my neck. A knit hat is snug on my head. Black tights and patent leather shoes cover little feet, poised and ready to hit the floor as soon as the doorbell rings. But it doesn't.

Hours pass. Sweat streams down my face. I ignore my mother's pleas to take off my coat. My daddy said he's coming. Her disbelief has nothing to do with my belief that he will. He said he's coming; all I have to do is wait.

So I do.

I wait until darkness turns to dawn. I wait until my clothes stick like adhesive tape to my skin. My mother carries my limp body to bed. She's outlasted my weeping, which has lulled me to sleep. The next morning, I awaken confused. My daddy didn't come. For reasons I wanted more than anything to understand and forgive, he simply didn't show.

There were more days like this, many more. Each time, the pain of his absence left a scar uglier than the last. He was my dad, the man I longed to know—the first man I ever loved and hoped would love me back. Whether we were driving around in his super-cool white Pontiac Grand Prix with the sunroof open or listening to Marvin Gaye, just being in his presence was something like magic to me. But when he didn't show, time after time, I wondered if it was because of me. And in my little-girl mind with a little-girl's dismay, I told myself I wasn't enough of anything for him and probably never would be.

My father's entry and exit continued for years. Sometimes he was around; most times he wasn't. Sometimes he kept his word; most times he didn't. His presence was like an imaginary door that he swung open and closed. When he opened it, the warmth of his love flowed through and blanketed me. But when he closed the door, it was impenetrable. No pleading or tears could pry it open.

My mother could no longer take it. If he continued his drifting, she'd take him to court for child support—something he'd always feared, something she'd never done before. And with no parting words or promises to return, my father simply closed the door one last time and disappeared.

I never blamed my mother. She rescued me. Even though I sometimes wondered where he was, I no longer expected him to be there for me. His absence, as hurtful as it was, neutralized the suspense of seeing if he'd finally show up and be the father I'd always imagined him to be. He never did; he never was. And eventually, I stopped wondering.

Now here I stand in the same shoes as my mother, watching my son peer at a door that remains closed despite his hopes that it will one day open. It's a persistent pain a mother raising a son alone knows: the pain of watching your child's sky-high hopes come crashing down when the phone doesn't ring; the pain of his distress when Daddy delivers an apology instead of himself; the pain of your child standing by your side at a Father's Day celebration amid a sea of twinned fathers and sons. Those pains leave the deepest wounds. Like my mother did for me, I try to anesthetize them and give my boy relief.

At some point, a decision must be made: allow the door to swing open and closed, or nail it shut. Casualties are inevitable. One mother may decide the door will always be open. Another, like me, may decide she will no longer watch her child look for a ray of light to peek its way through the door's crack. She may one day decide to tear that door down and, in its stead, build a fortress that no longer allows access to her child's fragile feelings and tender heart. She will grant herself the grace that she has done her best for her child in the worst of circumstances. She'll remember her own childhood and know that when one door closes, another always opens. She'll rest assured that for this mother and this son, kindred in their fatherless-child fates, life and love will see them through.

Notes to My Autistic Daughter

Marianne Peel Forman

I. You are three and have not spoken,
except for *minna minna minna*
over and over again.

I study sign language
for *mama* and *thank you* and *please*
talking to you with my fingertips and words.

Paired like good wine and cheese
or peanut butter and jelly,
I invite you to come to this talking table.

II. In my every night dreams,
I brush my fingers under my chin, then under yours.
You follow my fingers with your eyes

and I see you mouth *thank you*
soundless communicating
with language on lips, minus the air to propel the words.

You sign *please*
and take my hand,
pulling me into a meadow

of blue-petalled flowers
and baby's breath
under a full and vibrating moon.

You sign *dance*
and climb onto my feet,
swaying us in the moonlight.

III. In our awake world,
I place the dusty contents of a Kool-Aid package
on your lips and mine.

I am inches from your face,
licking the Kool-Aid off my lips,
urging you to engage lips and tongue and teeth.

But your eyes are glassy and far away,
in a world I cannot see.
I pry a floor-length mirror off the wall,

plop you in my lap,
face us toward the mirror
and lick my lips again,

making cooing, smacking sounds,
delighting in the gritty sweetness on my lips.
Your jaw is set and firm.

No amount of *mmmm good*
will convince you to taste your own lips.
You are wandering in a faraway place.

And so I hold you
close against my soft places,
singing *minna minna minna*

along with you,
following your lead,
rocking to the rhythms you compose.

I Was the Different One

Nisa Rashid
as told to Regina R. Robertson

My birthday is in April, which is also National Poetry Month. In 2011, when I turned eleven, I decided to write eleven poems to celebrate both occasions. One of my poems, which I entitled, "While I'm Alive, I Will," read more like a bucket list. It included eight things that I hoped to do before I die, like ride a unicorn to Alaska, marry my love on a Mediterranean wave, and even dye my hair neon green. I also wrote that I wanted to walk a Brooklyn street with my father.

I was so young when I wrote that poem. I was optimistic and tended to fantasize about what might be possible, especially when it came to my father. Back then, I didn't really understand what deportation meant. I didn't realize that when he was sent to Guyana in 2009, when I was nine, it meant that he would not be allowed to come back to the United States. If he wasn't allowed to come back to the States, then he wouldn't be able to stop by his old block in the Bronx, and he definitely couldn't come see me in Brooklyn. I also didn't know that there was another option—that I could visit him in his homeland and walk down a street with him there.

I always knew that he had been in prison, but I was never embarrassed about him being my father. What was embarrassing for me was knowing that my friends and I didn't have the same type of home lives. A lot of them lived with their dads, and, because I sometimes talked about mine, they'd ask me why he was never around when they came over. I didn't know how to answer their questions, so I'd always find a way to make light of the fact that he wasn't there at that moment. I knew I was the different one, which was hard for me to admit and accept when I was a little girl.

When I was seven, my mother and I went out with a friend of mine, along with his mother. While we were eating, our mothers shared that both of our fathers were serving time in prison. I immediately felt a sense of relief. Before that day, I had no idea that there were other people, and definitely not somebody I knew, in the same situation. Knowing that I wasn't alone helped me feel much more comfortable talking about my father.

As much as I used to avoid going into detail about his whereabouts, my father being in prison was never really a secret. My mother had written books and articles about their relationship and about our life, so many people knew the story. When I was growing up, I don't remember anybody talking about him or the situation too much, though. My mom's friends might ask, "Oh, how's your dad doing?" or something like that, but nobody ever asked me questions like, "Oh my God, how does it feel to not have a father?" Sometimes I would feel bad that he wasn't with me, physically, but I never felt like I didn't have a father. We have a great relationship, and he's always had a very strong presence in my life. I've always had my father.

I haven't seen him, in person, for a while, not since before he was deported, but we are still very close. We talk twice a week, and also stay in touch through social media. We Skype sometimes, too. I still remember when my mother and I would wake up early to drive or take the bus to go visit him. For me, those were always such happy times because I got to see him and spend time with him, but my mother used to tell me how mean the officers were to her, especially when I was a baby. She'd tell me that they were really horrible to her and made her feel uncomfortable during those visits, but I don't remember any of that.

My mother didn't tell me everything about his incarceration when I was growing up, but I think she was as honest as she could be. Even though she didn't outright say why he was serving a twenty-year sentence, she never painted him as a criminal either. Instead, she'd talk about the type of man he was. She always told me that he was a good person and that he didn't have the proper support or guidance around him when he was younger. That, along with his surroundings, was a big part of the reason why he was sent to prison as a teenager. He's made that clear to me, too.

If I had to describe my father in a few words, I would say that he is very protective and extremely caring. He always tells me how much he loves me, and, as I'm maturing, he talks to me about boys—"Be careful!"—just as any father would with his daughter. He sees my grades and hears all about my accomplishments from my mom, but one of the hardest and most confusing things about not living under the same roof with him is that he hasn't been able to see me grow, firsthand. I can tell that he knows I'm doing well because he always reminds me that I'm a smart, beautiful young lady. He's very encouraging and always wants the best for me. I know that, too.

I should also mention that my father is really religious. He grew up Catholic but converted to Islam when he went to prison, before he and my mother got married. When I was born, I was given two Arabic names—Nisa means "the woman" and Rashid means "the guide"—but I don't identify as Muslim, which is something I've expressed to him. He has tried to tell me that having one parent who is Muslim technically makes me Muslim, too, but I don't agree with him about that. As much as I respect his choice, I don't like some of the practices of his religion, especially as it relates to sexism. I know that Muslim women are supposed to cover their hair and things like that, but I don't support that. My mother is much more liberal and understanding.

We might not see eye-to-eye on religion, but my father and I are definitely connected by culture. His family is from Guyana, so, like him, I strongly identify with Guyanese culture. Living in New York, where so many cultures are appreciated, I am surrounded by Caribbean people in my neighborhood, and I am also in touch with my roots through food and music. I've taken it upon myself to read about Guyana and study its history, and my mom says that when I'm sixteen, we can take a trip so that I can see the country for myself. I look forward to that, but most of all, I look forward to seeing my father and walking down the street with him, hand in hand. I think we'll both be happy on that day. Until then, I will try to stay open and optimistic.

Growing up with a parent in prison was not an ideal situation, but as I get older, I understand how important it is to work with what you have. As thankful as I am to have such a wonderful father, I also know that it wasn't easy for my mother to carry so much of the weight of taking care of me. I appreciate her for all she's done. While we've had help from my grandparents and many friends, I think that running a household and raising a child is too much for one person to take on.

A lot of people ask me about my outlook on marriage and family, and I always say that I'd definitely like to have both. I see myself being married in the future and my husband will be at home. That last part is nonnegotiable. Maybe I'll even marry my love on a Mediterranean wave, just as I'd envisioned when I was eleven years old, when I wrote that poem. We shall see.

Nothing's better than the sound of little ones cracking up at something funny.

—Charlize Theron

Return

Dorianne Laux

My daughter, ten and brown—another summer
in Arizona with her father—steps
nonchalantly down the ramp as planes
unfurl their ghostly plumes of smoke.
I had forgotten how his legs, dark
and lean as hers, once strode toward me
across a stretch of hammered sand.
And her shoulders, sloped like his, a cotton
blouse scooped so low I can see
her collarbones arched gracefully
as wings, the cruel dip
in the hollow of her throat. And my throat
closes when she smiles, her bangs
blown into a fan around her face, hair
blond as the pampas grass that once waved
wild behind our fence. Whatever held us

together then is broken, dishes
in pieces on the floor, his dead
cigarettes crushed one after another
into the rail of the porch.
Now she opens her arms as he
used to, against a backdrop of blue sky,
so wide I worry she'll float up on these
gusts of clutching wind and disappear,
like a half-remembered dream, into
the perilous future, into the white
heart of the sun.

Teaching My Son to Write: An Abecedarian

Stacia Fleegal

For Jax

Alphabet no Andes for my
Big boy: bold and brilliant, he
Climbs the curves of cawing centuries to
Dear mom me someday, or describe the deer
Enjoying our endive, or emote, ego-stroke
(Fine!), to fan the flames of his feral, fragile self as
Good writers have for generations. God's sake,
He's five, I have half an hour to honor our heritage as
Instigating idealists before *Ice Age* starts again!
Justify: his J unjumbling is a jasmine blossom,
Kiss of a king bed after a killer day. It's a

Legacy thing, love and language, his linearity away from
Me already, meandering em dash. A mother
Needs this narcissistic nepotism
Or what oceanic oath is
Procreation? Passing on my passion, its practical and
Quixotic arms, its quaking and quiet qualms, its
Release, roar, revolution, is redemption.
Sit a second more, sweetheart, we're soon
Through with tonight's treatise, both
Ululating our understanding: you're
Very good at directions, I'm vehement that
Writing is a whole half of my worth, but your *J-A-*
X is my life's axis,
Your lion yawn, your bear hug, your
Zeal for knowing, my zen.

It's Really Not a Big Deal

Jacob Kronenberg

Dear Teacher,

I have an unusual family, and that can sometimes pose challenges. Not so much for us—we're happy as can be—but for other people wondering about us. I wanted to let you know the logistics to avoid some awkward questions: I have two moms. They were never married because same-sex marriage wasn't legal back then, but they split up when I was six, and now they're raising my sister and me together, but as separated solo moms. Both of my moms are equally my legal guardians. So they can both sign permission slips, call me in sick, and go to parent-teacher conferences. My sister and I live with both of them and split our time between their houses.

Please try not to make a big deal out of it in class. Because it's really not that big a deal. Assisted reproductive technology is nothing new, and plenty of straight married couples use it to have children. The separated and coparenting setup isn't terribly rare, either. And even though gay parents have made it into the mainstream with shows like *Modern Family*, a lot of kids (and, surprisingly, many adults) simply aren't aware of families like mine. Even people who might be fine with same-sex parents or a divorced mom parenting sometimes think it's weird when those two things are combined.

Another common response is the well-intentioned barrage of questions I get from friends or adults. Worse is when my totally normal family makes people act like I'm "the most interesting person in the world" and grill me about what it's like to be raised by two women. I do my best to be patient since it's often innocent curiosity, but it's sometimes hard to answer the same questions over and over again. The reason that I get tired of people making a big deal out of my family is that I really don't feel like it's as different as people think. I still have caring, supportive parents, and I grew up like any other kid.

If other kids are wondering how a family like mine works, I'd be happy to talk to them about it, but please don't make me address it in front of the whole class, especially not in a first-day get-to-know-you game, a genetics exercise on inherited eye color, or a French lesson on *La Famille et Les Parents*. I'm just like any other kid; please don't turn my normal life into a special lesson. The same goes for kids who might make fun of me or use bad language when talking about my family. I'll talk to them first and come get you if I need help.

Another thing you should know: like a lot of other moms, both of my moms work busy schedules, so sometimes other people might pick me up from school. These other people might include my mom's new girlfriend or my friend's parents. Please don't call my mom's girlfriend my mom, and don't ask if my friend's dad is my dad. I was born with a donor, so I don't have a dad at all. If you don't know who someone is, don't assume—just ask! I won't mind at all!

To me, the most important thing about my family has nothing

to do with the fact that I have two moms or that I was conceived with a donor. It has everything to do with our tradition of having crepes for breakfast or singing along to the *Sound of Music* on road trips. If you have any questions, feel free to ask me, my mom, or my mom.

Thanks,
Jacob

An Open Letter to Our Sperm Donor

Robin Silbergleid

Our daughter looks like me
    people say, the architecture
of her eyebrows and pointed stare.
    But in the photograph of you
at thirteen months: our baby's
    toothless grin after she's grabbed
the cat by the tail. Every child
    you said needs a mother who reads
and each night I let her suck
    thick cardboard illustrations,
Big Red Barn and *Goodnight Moon*,
    while I balance her on my lap.
If you lived with us, you
    would know this. Perhaps
you would bring me a cup of tea
    while I nurse her on the couch,

a book of poems open nearby.
    Sometimes I wonder if you wonder
about us, when you're at work
    in the laboratory or when
you're feeding your new son a bottle.
    The stories of our children
are woven together. The tapestry
    couldn't be more beautiful, filled
with these widening holes.

Dad Day:
Death Is a Holiday

Lennlee Keep

Almost a year had passed since my ex-husband, Josh, was found dead. As the anniversary approached, I felt pressure from friends and family to mark the occasion. My son and I had spent an entire year trying to regain shreds of normalcy and happiness. The idea of revisiting our loss with a date circled on the calendar seemed agonizing and dumb. It would be like swimming in a lightning storm. Sure, you might not get struck and drown, but why would you risk it?

Plus, there were practicalities. Since Josh was "found" dead after a long battle with alcoholism, we didn't know the exact date of his death. We couldn't spend the day visiting his grave because he was cremated and his ashes were in our living room. I suppose we could've held a vigil next to the bookcase where the urn sits, but that seemed weird.

What I knew for sure was that I couldn't ignore the day. I didn't want my son, Dash, to look back years later and wonder why we hadn't done anything for that first anniversary. I never wanted Dash to think that I had forgotten his dad or didn't love him, even though we had been divorced for three years before he died.

Sobbing over photos and focusing on Josh's absence would have been an awful way to spend the day. I'm also not a big fan of the otherwise popular "celebration of life" thing, because of the way it erases our sadness. I think people should be allowed to grieve in all its complexity. I hated hearing, "He would have wanted you to be happy—he wouldn't want you to cry." First of all, that negates the pain of our loss, and second, if Josh could have whatever he wanted, I'll bet that he would have wanted not to be dead.

So I created Dad Day—a day when Dash and I do everything his father would have loved. Josh was British and loved Marmite, so we "eat" it for breakfast. We don't really eat it, because it is a disgusting yeast paste that neither of us can stand. But we smear it on toast, take a bite, gag, then run to the sink to spit it out. After that, we stick to Josh's other favorites: pizza, Dr Pepper, popcorn, and gummy bears.

Josh was a huge hockey fan, so we bust out his New York Rangers jerseys. Dash wears the white one all day, and I wear the blue one for as long as I can stand it. My God, the polyester! We watch cricket, which neither of us understands, and Josh's favorite movies, like *The Warriors*, then finish the day with as many episodes of *The Simpsons* as time allows.

Stories about Josh naturally come up. I tell Dash about the time he threw a big party while his parents were out of town. He would have gotten away with it if he hadn't recorded a lot of it on the answering machine. Or the time he met Margaret Thatcher and accidentally dropped a condom at her feet. Her response was, "Well? Pick it up then!"

Josh's brother Max calls from Italy and shares more wild tales, like the Christmas they outran the police in Zanzibar, or the time Josh sent his six-year-old brother Louie home alone in a London taxi because he wanted to spend some time with a cute girl he had just met. We laugh about what a crazy teenager he was. And yes, we cry a little, because Josh would have loved Dad Day, and he's missing it.

Joshua Keep was born on April 21, 1969, and was found dead on August 19, 2016. But he wasn't just his delivery and expiration dates. He was his smile. He was the way he laughed and gave and yawned and worked and loved. I want to give Dash the intimate pieces of the man he can never know in this way. I try to breathe life back into Josh through stories and myths of his heroism, his stupidity, and his kindness.

So once a year on our fake holiday, we shine light on the person he was. We pull him back to us. All of the things and the people he loved are still here. We show him how much we remember—and how little we can forget.

I was lucky to be in the shadow of a giant. My mom's magic dust sprinkled on me, and I hope I have enough to be as brave as she was and continues to be.

—Trevor Noah

How to Pray

Sage Cohen

I follow two steps behind my son
on the gravel path as he shouts

hello to ducks. The squirrel has lost
a stripe of fur down his back.

I should have married someone else.
A person can die of motherhood.

Even the flame maple's promises
have stopped sleeping in the house.

He was gone years before he was
gone. First, he shot a doorway

through me, one complaint at a time.
Then he stepped through the place

my body once was and kept going.
He said he wanted to keep

trying, but what did that mean
in the absence of trying?

God, the cherry blossoms are in bloom.
This morning my son made me

an arrangement of flowers shredded
with scissors. I married a man

whose hands were unmade to please me.
I hold the vase like a torch.

Butterfly and Sunshine

Marika Lindholm

The blue bird with the black wings floated for a moment in midair, as if just as stunned as we were that she'd escaped through the bathroom window of our fourth-floor walk-up. My daughter and I caught this pause, and then the parakeet she'd named Butterfly was gone. We stared at the tarred rooftops and the fire escapes, and both burst into tears.

When I moved five-year-old Ella and her three-year-old brother, Jonas, out of the house where we lived with their father, my guilt propelled me to make our small apartment as comforting as possible. I gave each child a room of their own. I slept on the couch. Too much of my paycheck helped create a bold, dinosaur-themed room for my son, while my daughter's walls, sheets, blankets, and pillows were festooned with purple and pink butterflies. The tiny blue parakeet, which I purchased at PetSmart after a particularly devastating mediation session during which her father accused me of destroying his life, was my latest nod to Ella's obsession and my bottomless guilt.

The three of us combed city blocks, called up into trees, and told every passerby that our pet bird had flown away. A few took pity on us, suggesting we call local vets and make posters. We kept walking. Tears rolled down Ella's cheeks, while Jonas whined that his feet hurt. I wanted to fall to the ground and bang my head against the sidewalk to make the pain go away. Dusk came, and we finally had to give up.

A therapist had counseled us on how to break the news of our divorce. A script was written. It was suggested that since the kids were so young, it was best to wait until only a few days before we moved out. Apparently, it wouldn't feel real to them until it happened—no kidding. The "divorce talk" unfolded as planned: We cried and hugged our children, and then he collected them in his arms and, over their embrace, fired an accusatory glare.

I'd prepared our new apartment for weeks, painting and decorating, while suffering humiliations such as asking my parents to cosign the lease and surreptitiously selling clothes, shoes, and sports equipment that wouldn't fit in my new home. That first day, I took a deep breath, held my children's hands, and walked them up the three flights of stairs with a forced smile. At the top of the stairwell, I kneeled down, panting, pulled them close, and said, "I know this is weird and sad, but I promise that I will spend every day trying to make you happy." They smiled bravely, and we stepped into our new life.

Ella painstakingly cut and glued photos of Butterfly for a poster, and we made 100 copies of it at the library. Jonas watched *The Backyardigans* while I called local animal specialists and veterinarians. How could I let this happen? Before taking Butterfly out of the cage, we always marched around shutting all the windows. But this time I forgot the barely open bathroom window behind the shower curtain. The speed at which Butterfly found this tiny exit haunted me.

Ella and I hit the streets the next morning. That damn bird. Every glint of blue sent my heart racing. Could it be?

Once the posters were distributed, Ella asked, "Do you think Butterfly has new friends?"

The repercussions of moving out were swift. My angelic three-year-old boy with a head full of golden curls now kicked my car seat, hurled food, and smashed toys. His tantrums quickly became legendary, often ending in choking noises or no noise at all when he passed out from crying. The first time it happened, I was certain he'd died.

Ella dutifully reported that group therapy was helpful, and she gave me hugs when Jonas refused to cooperate. We did the dishes together, hauled laundry to the laundromat, and made photo albums of our new life. Yay, pumpkins! Yippee, the playground! Wow, a new school! Look at us three having fun! Many a page was dedicated to Butterfly, perched on Ella's finger, shoulder, and, of course, on top of her head.

Two days after we put up the posters, a woman called and said, "I think we have your parakeet."

"What?!"

Across town, in a real house with a beautiful lawn, a portly, long-haired woman invited us in and told us the story of the sweet bird that had showed up in her apple tree. Ella and I laughed at our tremendous good fortune and walked toward the large bamboo cage. The only inhabitant was a yellow parakeet with black wings.

"That's not Butterfly!" Ella cried.

How could we have missed that detail—the bird's color—in

our conversations? I bit my lip and held back the tears that Ella let so freely fall.

"Honey, I'm sorry this isn't your parakeet, but you can have it." Did the kind woman sense the fragility of the situation, or did she just want to get rid of the bird?

Ella's eyes widened.

"It's very friendly, and you can even have this lovely cage."

An intricate bamboo replica of the Taj Mahal, the cage barely fit in our car. I heard Ella coo from the back seat, "I'm going to name you Sunshine." Then she whispered, "Don't ever think about flying away."

My first winter on the couch was filled with many new challenges, but none were as frustrating as trying to find a parking spot close enough to our apartment from which an exhausted preschooler and kindergartener could make it to the building and then up all those stairs. Too often, I took risks that I'm not proud of—leaving them in the foyer, asking a sketchy neighbor to keep watch, or locking them in the car while I ran bags of groceries upstairs.

A Chicago snowstorm was my undoing. I double-parked, put the kids in the foyer, and promised a hasty return. Most street parking was forbidden to allow for snow removal. With snow pounding my windshield, I searched and searched for a place to put the car. Without snow tires, the car slipped and slid as I inched block by block looking for a spot. Panic rose in my throat as I circled a two-block, three-block, and finally five-block radius. Not a damn spot in sight.

If I'd just stuck it out in my marriage, my babies wouldn't be waiting in a steamy foyer, wondering if their mother would ever come back. Trying to regulate my breathing, I pleaded with fate: keep my kids safe, and I will never leave them alone again. But no matter how much I bargained, it was useless.

Berating myself for putting my own happiness ahead of my children, I ditched the car in a snowdrift and ran toward home as large, wet snowflakes smacked me in the face. I fumbled with the lock and, to my enormous relief, found Ella reading *One Fish, Two Fish, Red Fish, Blue Fish* to Jonas. I pulled them close and said through my sobs, "I'm so sorry. Mommy is really sorry." They looked up at me as if I was out of my mind—because I was.

Sunshine turned out to be an unusually social parakeet whom we all came to adore. He wanted to cuddle and stay close. All of us benefited from the joyful yellow bird resting in our arms as we watched TV or sitting on a shoulder during homework. Over time, we made new friends, created our own family rituals, and learned to love our small apartment above the treetops. Sunshine's joyful trill provided the soundtrack as we found our rhythm as a family of three, in which recrimination and guilt were replaced by relief and laughter.

Almost two years later, we noticed that Sunshine's left wing had started to droop. His flying became clumsy and unreliable. A tumor was to blame, and it was terminal.

Those last weeks, he never used his fancy cage, but slept on Ella instead. My fear of him getting crushed was unfounded.

One weekend when the kids were at their dad's house, I sensed the end was near and moved into Ella's room. I wanted to make Sunshine comfortable, but he didn't want any of it. He somehow made it into a corner under a table, his tiny chest heaving with the effort of breathing. It felt intrusive and disrespectful to watch him, but every fifteen minutes I would crawl on my hands and knees to see if he'd passed.

After many hours, Sunshine was trembling spasmodically. Why was this taking so long? I decided that enough was enough. I gave him a full dropper of children's acetaminophen. Within minutes, he died in my hand.

The house was quiet. It was too late to call the children. I wrapped the seemingly weightless body in a kitchen towel and sat for a long time before gathering my gloves, coat, and a spade. In the dark of night, I dug a hole for the yellow parakeet who had come into our life when we were fragile and in pain. As I spilled dirt over him, tears flowed, and my heart ached. But unlike on the day Butterfly disappeared, I was actually crying about Sunshine, whose joyful chirping and chattering made us smile. The next day Ella, Jonas, and I would return to this spot for a proper funeral. Words were said and tears fell, but at this moment, as I patted down the dank earth and arranged small stones in the shape of a heart, I knew that although our sweet bird would be missed, the three of us were going to be alright.

Chapter Two:
Lean on Me

In truth, I am a single mother. But I don't feel alone at all in parenting my daughter. Krishna has a whole other side of her family who loves her, too. And so Krishna is parented by me, but also by her grandmother and aunts and cousins and uncles and friends.

—Padma Lakshmi

Finding My Voice, Feeding My Friends

Janelle Hardy

"Don't let them push you around. Make sure you ask for Cynthia when you call the office."

My friend Monife, a fellow grad student and refugee from Nigeria, was coaching me on self-advocacy.

A shy, quiet solo mom, I had little experience asserting myself. But I had reached the limit of my resources. I had no choice.

At age twenty-four, with an eleven-month-old baby, I had moved 5,500 kilometers from my northern Canadian home to study for my master's degree in Toronto. I knew that I could afford school only if I received a subsidy for my daughter's daycare. Immediately after we arrived in Toronto, I had enrolled my daughter in the university's spectacularly diverse cooperative daycare and then applied for the city's subsidy program.

"Where are you from?" the caseworker asked.

"The Yukon."

She looked through my financial statements and circumstances. A solo mother, far from home, with student loans, a part-time university job, and limited resources—I most definitely qualified for the subsidy.

"How are you paying for daycare?" she demanded.

In 2003, the monthly rate for an infant was $950. I couldn't afford it. But I had used my credit card to pay for the first month while I waited for my subsidy application to be processed.

"My credit card?" My whisper curved into a question.

"I don't believe you. You're too broke." With that announcement, she sent me on my way. Subsidy denied.

I didn't say a word.

On the city bus, heading back to the university, I swallowed my tears and calculated that I could afford two more months of daycare before I'd have to quit school and return north. I didn't appeal the decision. I didn't question it. I don't think I even spoke to anyone about the unfairness of it. Instead, I silently despaired, churning the details over and over in my mind, trying to figure it out.

Until I met Monife, a solo mom who volunteered at the daycare office. Monife had already been through the wringer of applications, bureaucracy, and culture shock. She'd learned the ins and outs of big city solo motherhood, and she was not at all interested in acquiescing to unfair decisions.

One day she asked me, in her characteristically straightforward way, what kind of daycare subsidy I was getting, assuming it was 100 percent. When I shared that I was paying the full monthly fee myself, she was outraged. She fumed with horror stories about the subsidy office and their caseworkers. Then she told me, "You have to go back and appeal the decision."

An appeal? I was floored. Was that possible? I had no sense of agency and very little faith that I could make myself heard. But I also desperately longed to stay in school, and I was almost entirely out of money. So I followed Monife's advice. I booked another appointment.

Sitting on a fabric-covered office chair that was meant to appear cozy, clenching my knees tightly together, resisting the urge to sob every time words left my mouth, I told Cynthia, the caseworker Monife had recommended, what happened the first time I applied for a subsidy.

"She said what!?" Cynthia cried. "That is absolutely appalling! How have you been paying for daycare? I can't believe this happened to you. I'm going to fix it."

I took trembly breaths, wiping driblets from the corners of my eyes as relief flooded through me.

"You qualify for a full subsidy," she explained. "We're not usually allowed to do back pay, but this is outrageous."

Within a week, my daycare fee shrunk from $950 a month to $50 a month, and the three months I'd already paid for were reimbursed. My first lesson in self-advocacy came from a solo mom.

Over the course of my two years in Toronto, I collected several solo mom friends. Monife was raising a son by a Nigerian man. Elsa, from Sweden, was raising a daughter by a Jamaican man. Annette, from Jamaica, was raising a son by a Nigerian man. I was raising a daughter by a Barbadian man. We were all doing our master's degrees (in environmental studies, biology, business, and dance, respectively). We were all raising children of mixed race and culture, without the other parents' involvement or support. We were all in some degree of culture shock and adjustment.

My individual friendships with these women evolved into a semiweekly potluck feast. I would roast a lemony herb chicken and invite my friends and their little ones over for a meal. I loved the din of happy children playing in my tiny apartment above the campus daycare. I loved the scent of the food—the chicken, roasted veggies, store-bought crackers and cheese, and sometimes wine. I loved the roar of laughter rising out of the circle of women seated on the floor with our toddlers, plates of food balanced, teetering, on our knees.

This is how I survived being a solo mother, in school, with a tiny daughter: by stumbling into a tribe of solo mother friends. We were kindred spirits, keenly intelligent, adventurous, fierce, and generous with information. These friends helped me grow into an independent woman who stands up for herself and her daughter. They helped me grow into a woman who knows the hunger for sisterhood and knows how to cultivate it. My solo mother friends reached out with kindness, food, childcare, and advice. In turn, I learned how to reach back, how to pass on that knowledge, and, most importantly, how to self-advocate, onwards.

For My Sisters

Sharisse Kimbro

This is for my sisters
not the back-stabbing, gossip-grabbing,
"who does she think she is" sisters,
not the success-hating, man-stealing,
"I can't stand that b—" sisters,
not the smile in your face, talk behind your back sisters,
not the tell your business to anyone who will listen sisters,
not the hating, berating, and manipulating sisters,
not the pretense without purpose sisters,
not the image with no substance sisters,
no, this is for the *real* sisters . . .

the . . .
. . . I will stand with you when the world is against you sisters
. . . I will hold you up when you can stand no longer sisters
. . . your secret is safe with me sisters
. . . I will tell you the truth even when it hurts sisters

the . . .
. . . I will hold your feet while you give birth to your destiny sisters
. . . I won't be jealous when your promise comes sisters
. . . I'll show you how to nurse a vision so it won't hurt sisters

the . . .
. . . I'll be at your door with some greens and macaroni and cheese
when you've lost a loved one sisters
. . . I will drive through the night to sit next to you
at your momma's funeral sisters
. . . I will go through her clothes for you sisters
. . . I won't hang up the phone when you call me crying sisters

the . . .
. . . I will hold your hand when you receive the diagnosis sisters
. . . I will drive you home from chemo sisters
. . . I will shave my head too sisters
. . . I will weep with you because I lost my mother sisters
. . . I will weep with you because I am a mother sisters

the . . .
. . . I will ask the hard questions sisters
. . . I won't tell you what you want to hear, but what you need to sisters
. . . I will cut a *brotha* if he lays one hand on you sisters
. . . I will come and get you and won't give him the chance
to do it again sisters
. . . I will send you a plane ticket so that you can escape sisters
. . . I will treat a broken spirit and a bruised heart
like I would a broken arm and a black eye sisters

the . . .
. . . I will wait with you until he comes home sisters
. . . I won't let you confront him alone sisters
. . . I will sit with you in court all day sisters
. . . I'll treat you the same when it's over sisters

the . . .
. . . I will be praying on the other end of the phone
when you call me bleeding from a miscarriage sisters
. . . I will wake up in the middle of the night and pray
when you haven't called
because I feel you bleeding in the spirit sisters
. . . I will come and find you when you are sitting in the car
with the garage door closed and the ignition on sisters
. . . I will lay with you on the floor sisters
. . . I will pick you up off the floor sisters

the . . .
. . . I will wear that ugly-ass dress and be happy about it
at your wedding sisters
. . . I will celebrate with you because you are "the bomb!" sisters
. . . I will sing with you because I am really happy that you are happy
and your success is my success sisters

the . . .
. . . I will forgive you when you mess up sisters
. . . I will help you forgive yourself sisters
. . . I love you in spite of you sisters
. . . I love you because of you sisters

Yes, this is for my sisters—the real sisters
who know the most important thing we can do
is simply be there, sisters.

from A Beautiful, Terrible Thing

Jen Waite

I run now. Every day. Something I never thought I would say. I run, not away from the past but toward the future. Every morning I breathe in Lulu's sweet baby smell as I put her down for her morning nap, the one I can always count on for at least an hour around 9 a.m., and I throw on my running clothes, lace up my bright-orange sneakers, and fly out the front door. I still don't know exactly what I am running toward, but it feels good to move, to sweat, to feel my muscles straining and working. A few months ago, in the depths of the chaos and depression, my skinniest pair of pre-pregnancy jeans hung from my frame. But now I have gained back some weight, my skin glows with the summer sun, and although my stomach is soft and saggy where it used to be hard and taut, I look in the mirror and see that I look the best I have ever looked. My lips turn up in a small smile at the irony of this. I turn from the mirror and run down the stairs, wave to my mom, and head out the front door and then stop. I run back inside, grab my car keys, and yell, "Going to run some errands, be back in an hour."

Forty-five minutes later, I stare at the woman across from me. Her blonde hair hangs in a full bob just past her chin, and her eyes are clear and wise.

"What do you think?" the sleek red-headed stylist asks from behind the chair.

"I love it," I say, touching the smoothness of my hair. Suddenly, I am transported back to the bar, that first night with Marco, and I think of that girl twirling her hair nervously around her finger.

"Are you sure? You look a little sad," the stylist says with a concerned laugh.

"No, I do. I love it. Thank you." My hand goes to my hair again, and I give it a soft pat. "I was just thinking about how much there used to be."

"You needed a change, my dear."

"You have no idea."

Tonight I nurse my daughter to sleep. I poke the corner of her mouth gently with my finger to loosen her grip on my nipple, and she pulls away with a start. Her eyes open for a second, and one arm flails out to the side. Suddenly, for the first time, I see her. It is like I have taken off smudgy glasses that I didn't even know I was wearing. "You're so beautiful," I say in awe. "I see you." She has sandy, light-brown hair and the most beautiful blue, almond-shaped eyes I have ever seen. She smiles at me, and I say again, "Oh my God, I see you." The haze of grief that has enveloped me for six months lifts for a moment. I touch her cheek with my finger. I make a soothing, shushing sound and kiss the top of her head. Her hair smells like honey and baby, and for a moment she is the whole world and there is nothing else. I kiss her again and lay her in her crib and tiptoe out of the room, holding my breath as the door creaks in the same spot that it always creaks.

Once I'm back in my bedroom, my phone stares at me from my bedside table, beckoning me. I haven't checked either of their profiles all day. Don't do it. Don't do it. But now my fingers are moving independently from my body, typing and swiping and shaking just a tiny bit. *He can't hurt me anymore. He can't hurt me anymore. I don't even care.* This is what I tell myself. His profile shows nothing new, and my brain barely absorbs this before my fingers are already pressing and swiping toward her profile. Her profile loads, and I see she has posted a new picture. A mixture of fear, adrenaline, anxiety, and nausea mingle in my stomach as I tap once and the new picture fills the screen. And then my eyes focus, and I see . . . she is wearing my husband's pajamas. Ex-husband. Exexexex, get it straight, Jenny. The pajamas I bought him two Christmases ago and bought matching pairs for my dad and my sister's husband. Red and green and white stripes. Marco wore them Christmas Day and then they became his day-off pants. We would sit on the couch with Chinese takeout from across the street, him in those pj's and me in my moccasin slippers. And after we had finished our greasy meal, I would lay my head in his soft, flannel lap. A pit opens up in my heart. So now I know he can still hurt me. As I examine the picture, I feel a lump rising in my throat. I wait. The lump is still there, but I am not crying. *It's OK to cry*, I tell myself. Still, no tears. I click to my home screen and bring up my text messages.

"Croella posted a pic wearing pj's I bought Marco for Christmas. But I'm not crying."

Nat responded, "No way. Is there no limit to their asshole douchiness?? Like, NO LIMIT? But that's good. But it's OK to cry."

"I know, but now I need to stop looking. I am just digging at the wound. Need to change my behavior."

Yes. Progress. Suddenly, not crying when I see my husband's

girlfriend wearing the pajamas I bought him is a step in the right direction. I laugh out loud and close my eyes.

I walk through the aisles of Target pushing Lulu in her stroller. My mom and her sister, my aunt Julia, are meeting me to do a bit of shopping, and I have arrived a few minutes early. I walk slowly past racks of clothes, taking in the huge, empty store. After living in New York for nine years, I am still not used to having personal space in public, and I luxuriate in the unapologetic suburban consumerism.

"Oh look, Mags, I see them!" I hear the familiar ring of my aunt's voice travel from the entrance of the store to the rack of clothing where I am holding up a striped tank top against my body. She was one of the first people I told about the real reason I was home. After a month of my parents dodging questions about why Louisa and I were in Maine for such a long visit, she came over for coffee and donuts at the end of March. I sat with Louisa in a chair at the head of the dining table and nervously picked at the donut in front of me. "Aunt Julia, I have to tell you something," I said, swallowing down the lump in my throat. "The real reason I'm home with Louisa is because I found out Marco was having an affair when Louisa was a few weeks old, and I've moved home until I figure out what to do." I stared into my coffee, and when I looked up my aunt's face was bright red, tears streaming down her nose and cheeks. She sank into a chair, and for several minutes all she could get out was "What?" over and over. When I saw that she was crying, I let myself cry, too—big, ugly sobs. And then my mom started to cry and hugged my aunt.

"But your wedding was just a few months ago," my aunt finally said. "I don't understand."

"Join the club," I said with a small smile, drying my eyes with a napkin. I explained the email, the change in personality, his numbness, and the suicide attempt.

I had completely forgotten that when my cousin Luke was a baby, my aunt's abusive husband had disappeared one day with all their money and had never come back. She had remarried my uncle Sam a few years later, and everyone in our family had buried the first part of her story in a deep hole and thrown twenty years of new memories on top of it. She told me how hard the next few years would be but that I would be OK. "You have to grieve the family and the future you thought you would have. And you have to go through an entire cycle of holidays, birthdays, and seasons before you really stop feeling that raw pain. Even then, all the 'firsts' will be hard, the first time she sleeps in her crib, her first word, the first time she walks. But then one day you will wake up and you will be so glad it happened. And that it happened when she was a newborn. You will realize your lives are so, so much better without Marco, if this is really who he is."

I absorbed her words and stored them away, aware that I would need to draw on them one day.

There must be those among whom we can sit down and weep and still be counted as warriors.

—Adrienne Rich

Raising a Boy without a Man

Kathleen Laccinole

I am a single mother. Fifty percent of us are.

I have a son. Forty-nine-point-two of us do.

When he was born, I was in a quandary.

By month nine of my pregnancy, my baby's father already had one foot out the door, with the other right behind it. It was obvious I would be doing this solo.

Because nothing else in my *I Love Lucy* fantasy had actually come to be, I had decided to do the one traditional thing I could and wait to find out the sex of my baby. In my heart of hearts, though, I knew there was a girl curled up inside me, with polished nails, pink tights, and a tiara on her head.

I painted the nursery a soft yellow, an asexual apple tree on the wall. I stenciled a rocking chair in nonpartisan colors, bought pounds of blankets, rompers, and onesies in neutral shades. Still, I had ballet dancer dolls and ruffled socks hidden in a drawer on standby.

It was time. My mom, sister, and BFF held my hand, shouted encouragement, and squealed in delight as my baby, my *One Day At a Time* fantasy, slipped into the world . . . and had a penis.

The words fell from my mouth: "What the hell am I going to do with that?"

The doctor held up my son to show me his perfection, and he peed, a fountain of urine shooting from the firm, tiny stump between his slimy legs. Everyone laughed as my doctor pivoted side to side for effect, like the rotating sprinklers I'd run through as a child in my blue nylon bathing suit from Sears.

The nurses did what nurses do when babies are born, then put my son in my arms. He was tiny and funny looking. Precious. I loved him already. I'd name him William, after my grandfather. He was my dream come true. And he was a boy.

What the hell am I going to do?

The ballerina dolls and ruffled socks remained in the drawer. The choo-choo, cowboy, and rocketship everythings came rolling in. I swaddled, cuddled, nursed. We lived in a dreamy world of mother-son bliss. He'd sleep nestled in my armpit. The top of his head smelled like warm, sticky-sweet joy.

But then came the threes. Out went teddy bears and in came trucks, forts, action figures, and anything that could be construed as the forbidden gun: carrots, French fries, sticks, straws, or the good old-fashioned index finger, replete with sound effects masterfully manufactured by his wet, squishy mouth.

I had myself a boy. The type who'd need to wrestle, mud-stomp, play sports, stink, build, fish, invent, and ride rockets to the moon. I couldn't use a screwdriver. Who would teach my boy to be a man?

What the hell am I going to do?

I tried handymen. They fixed things that subsequently broke again because I didn't know how to choose handymen (like I couldn't choose men in general). My son fell in love with them nonetheless, following them around like a hungry puppy, wearing his My First Tool Belt with the plastic hammers and flaccid tape measure. But the jobs would end, and the handymen would leave, back to their own sons, my door still crooked, the sink still clogged, exposed wires calling my son's name.

I called in the lesbians. They showed up. They smelled good. They fixed things with an eye toward my son's safety. They taught him to use a real hammer and unplug a toilet. He fell in love. "I want to marry Lynda. But Lynda is married to Kelly." They loved him back. But they had vaginas, just like me.

What the hell am I going to do?

I tried to find role models on TV. We watched every *Andy Griffith Show*, then watched them again. When my son asked about sex, I asked myself, *What would Andy say to Opie?* I told him. He thought it was gross. We went for ice cream.

I hit up the usual suspects: Little League, Boy Scouts, teachers, and coaches. They ruffled his hair when he failed, scolded him when he was lazy, high-fived him when he succeeded. But he was just one of a million boys. Who would teach him the things a mom cannot? With whom could he dude joke, talk about girls, burp and fart, and ponder the universe?

What the hell am I going to do?

That's when, for lack of an after-school activity, we wandered into Val Surf, our local surf shop. From the moment we pushed through those doors stickered with snowboard, skateboard, and surfboard logos, our lives forever changed. The music blasted, the energy was relaxed, and the air smelled like coconuts. A blond, tan, sales stud welcomed my boy with a casual, "Hey, little man." My son's eyes widened, a smile spreading across his face. I'd found my village of father figures.

We'd visit the store once a week to wander the aisles of surf-boards, my son touching expressive designs on smooth, cool surfaces, no two alike. We marveled at the ever-changing wall of skateboards, floor-to-ceiling masterpieces, an installation to rival any museum. Balancing on the Indo board was a highlight. "I'm practicing for when I can surf," he'd say.

The staff helped my son select "cool" shorts and Vans, always in the correct size. When he bought his first skateboard, they told him to wear a helmet: "Be safe, little man." He learned to ollie, kickflip, and grind—hours and hours in our driveway.

Then it happened. On his thirteenth birthday, these young men taught my boy to surf.

Thanks to surf superstars the likes of Laird Hamilton and Kelly Slater, surf culture had shifted from fringe to clean living. For my son, this meant no drugs, no alcohol, juicing, sunscreen, look out for your bros in the water, and be cool to your mom.

When my son discovered his uncle was a lifelong surfer, the weekly Sunday morning surfs began, topped by evenings barbecuing, sitting in the hot tub, talking about fishing and surfing, and contemplating the universe. Then, my son would be delivered home to me exhausted, full of stories, happy, content.

Among this tribe, my son found a mentor: a wild-haired, surf-loving PhD in environmental health who taught him how to shape surfboards and implanted the importance of higher education. Oh, how I loved our long drives home from the workshop, my boy recounting every beat of the day, every joke, every word—precious time forever ours, forever connecting us in memories.

Now, at fifteen, his once sweet-smelling hair smacks of salt water, his skin brown, his life overflowing with remarkable men he looks up to and who look after him. The men who once called him "little man" and taught him how to be a grown one.

Fifteen years ago, I fancied myself a woman burned, jaded, and scorned. At that moment in time—when I'd lost all respect for 49.2 percent of the human race—I received what I needed most: a boy.

To raise my boy solo, I needed to meet him where he was in his boy-ness, to appreciate our differences, to follow him on his adventures to my bravest ability, and, when he exceeded my reach, to outsource the rest.

In the process, I've developed my own sense of confidence— strong enough to stand up to the towering six-foot-two child I am still raising, the child now strong enough to carry me when I break my foot, to fix my broken dryer, and to ease my broken heart with just a smile and a hug.

Somewhere along the way, I learned to respect men again, even admire them—the ones who earn it, at least. I can see the colorful positives in their quirks, foibles, exuberant humor, and, at times, their complete and utter frustrating cluelessness.

More importantly, I see my son's future as a compassionate, intelligent, hardworking, piss-your-pants funny, willing-to-do-the-dishes man. I see a man of honor. I see the best person I know.

How do you raise a boy without a man? What the hell do you do? You meet him where he is. You keep your eyes open, even when it's scary, even when it's under salty sea water. You find role models in unexpected places, in all shapes and sizes. Some may even be tan and blond and smell like coconuts.

September 17

from *Operating Instructions*

Anne Lamott

We slept for six straight hours and are up nursing now. There is milk everywhere. I go around looking like I've got a wet bathing suit on under my clothes. When Sam was six days old, I took him to my little Black church in Marin City, the church where I've been hanging out for four years now. I wandered in one day the year before I stopped drinking, because it was right next to the most fabulous flea market on earth, where I liked to spend time when I had terrible hangovers. I got into the habit of stopping by the church on Sundays but staying in the back, in this tense, lurky way, and leaving before the service was over because I didn't want people to touch me, or hug me, or try to make me feel better about myself. I had always pretty much believed in God, and I just naturally fell into worshiping and singing with them. Then after I got sober and started to feel okay about myself, I could stay to the end and get hugged. Now I show up and position myself near the door, and everyone has to give me a huge hug—it's like trying to get past the border patrol. Once I asked my priest friend, Bill Rankin, if he really believed in miracles, and he said that all I needed to do was to remember what my life used to be like and what it's like now. He said he thought I ought to change my name to Exhibit A.

Anyway, the first Sunday after Sam's birth, I kind of limped in with Peg beside me. I was holding Sam and she was holding my little inflated doughnut seat, and everyone was staring joyfully and almost broken heartedly at us because they love us so much. I walked, like a ship about to go down, to a seat in the back. But the pastor said, Whoa, whoa, not so fast—you come up here and introduce him to his new family. So I limped up to the little communion table in the front of the half circle of folding chairs where we sit, and I turned to face everyone. The pain and joy were just overwhelming. I tried to stammer, "This is my son," but my lip was trembling, my whole face was trembling, and everyone was crying. When I'd first started coming to the church, I couldn't even stand up for half the songs because I'd be so sick from cocaine and alcohol that my head would be spinning, but these people were so confused that they'd thought I was a child of God. Now they've seen me sober for three years, and they saw me through my pregnancy. Only one (white) man in the whole congregation asked me who the father was. Toward the end of my pregnancy, people were stuffing money into my pockets, even though a lot of them live on welfare and tiny pensions. They'd sidle up to me, slip a twenty into the pocket of my sweater, and dart away.

Anyway, after I introduced Sam to them and sat down on my doughnut seat in the front row with Peg, I really got into the service. The baby was sound asleep in my arms, and I stood for the first hymn feeling very adult—an actual mother, for God's sake—only to discover that the doughnut seat was stuck to my bottom, and milk was absolutely pouring out of my breasts. I was not yet secure enough to hold the baby with one hand, so I was cradling him in my arms and couldn't free up either hand to pull the doughnut seat off. So I stood there bent slightly forward, warbling away, with my butt jutting out and ringed by the plastic doughnut.

Prayer

Keetje Kuipers

Perhaps as a child you had the chicken pox
and your mother, to soothe you in your fever
or to help you fall asleep, came into your room
and read to you from some favorite book,
Charlotte's Web or *Little House on the Prairie*,
a long story that she quietly took you through
until your eyes became magnets for your shuttering
lids and she saw your breathing go slow. And then
she read on, this time silently and to herself,
not because she didn't know the story,
it seemed to her that there had never been a time
when she didn't know this story—the young girl
and her benevolence, the young girl in her sod house—
but because she did not yet want to leave your side
though she knew there was nothing more
she could do for you. And you, not asleep but simply weak,

listened to her turn the pages, still feeling
the lamp warm against one cheek, knowing the shape
of the rocking chair's shadow as it slid across
your chest. So that now, these many years later,
when you are clenched in the damp fist of a hospital bed,
or signing the papers that say you won't love him anymore,
when you are bent at your son's gravesite or haunted
by a war that makes you wake with the gun
cocked in your hand, you would like to believe
that such generosity comes from God, too,
who now, when you have the strength to ask, might begin
the story again, just as your mother would,
from the place where you have both left off.

The Godfather

Margot Kessler

"He'll be here," my daughter said. "He texted me and said he was on his way from the airport."

The rain stopped, and the evening sun glistened on the Hudson River running behind the restaurant my daughter had chosen for her graduation dinner. We took family photos while we waited for him.

"He's always late," her sister explained to the other waiting guests. "We've named a time zone after him."

They know their godfather so well. Miss one of their college graduation celebrations? Never. Ever since she and her sister could remember, my dear friend Peter had shown up for ballet and orchestra recitals, school open houses, parents' days, graduations, and birthday parties.

Peter and I were now the same age my father had been when he first met Peter all those years ago. "Why is he here?" my mother would mutter when Peter showed up during college summers to whisk me off to a concert in his dad's beat-up convertible. "What's the point of someone you're not dating being your date?"

"He's a good friend," I told my proper mother.

I had no idea then how good a friend he would become. We make promises to ourselves when we're younger. We think we know what direction we're taking. Rarely are we correct. Peter and I told ourselves our friendship would be different. And, in some ways, it has been. Our professional lives had no overlap, yet we stayed in contact. After years on the East Coast with his girlfriend, he moved to California. Then he attended my wedding with his handsome boyfriend. Though it sometimes felt like our past was all we had in common, he was the one I chose to be my children's godfather.

Several years into my marriage, I realized my husband was an alcoholic and asked Peter's then-boyfriend and future partner, a life coach, to help me. But Peter's partner died suddenly of an aneurysm two weeks before we planned to stage an intervention. That year was a bad one for both of us. Peter lost weight and threw himself into caring for his patients and medical research, while I lost weight concentrating on making sure my kids were safe during the messy divorce.

As we each struggled with our separate grief, there was one constant: he was my daughters' godfather. Busy and overwhelmed, we somehow managed to connect regularly. Peter was always late and then later still to whatever he had planned afterward. A snappy dresser, he used to show up in pressed pants and elegant shoes. After my two-year-old insisted on walking on his feet and sitting on his lap, he learned to wear jeans and older shoes.

People didn't understand Peter's connection to my daughters. Why was he on the contact list at their schools? Why was he allowed to show up and whisk them off for an adventure? There were always questions implying unsolicited advice from other parents. Who was he? Did he live with us? Why did the kids call him by his first name? Did I know who he was dating?

Peter was conscientious about not overstepping or trying to parent, but he was always there. He helped my elder child wrench out her wiggly baby tooth in the middle of a Picasso exhibit, while I took her sister to the bathroom. He took both girls prom dress shopping and guided them through several ear piercings. His approval, like his taste in clothes (clothes I *never* would have purchased for my tween or teen girls), is open-minded and unerring. He allowed my soon-to-be pre-med daughter to work in his laboratory for the summer and get a firsthand glimpse at medical research. He became the girls' permission slip, sounding board, and cheerleader. In the wake of their father's erratic communication, disappearances, and disappointments, Peter was consistent, present, and uniquely himself.

Recently, Peter visited my younger daughter at college in Ohio for her art installation. My daughter talked him through her installation's concept, and he listened carefully, reminding her of her first dress design eight years earlier. My daughter's friends reached out to Peter, excited to meet a man they had heard so much about. Doing the introductions, my daughter explained that this was her family. Her godfather and I shared a glance. Of course, we are.

Our table for ten was ready, and we sat down, leaving a place at the end. My daughter watched the door. Just as the waiter handed us our menus, her godfather arrived. "I almost didn't make it," he said, explaining that his flight had accidentally been booked for the following weekend. "But miss my goddaughter's graduation? Never." My daughter beamed.

the lost women

Lucille Clifton

i need to know their names
those women i would have walked with
jauntily the way men go in groups
swinging their arms, and the ones
those sweating women whom i would have joined
after a hard game to chew the fat
what would we have called each other laughing
joking into our beer? where are my gangs,
my teams, my mislaid sisters?
all the women who could have known me,
where in the world are their names?

We Are Loved

Amy Rivers

The world is a blur.

Every morning when I open my eyes, I sense my surroundings in the shadows because they are familiar, not because I can see them. Blurry has been my reality since I was nine years old and diagnosed with a severe visual impairment brought on by rheumatoid arthritis. In elementary school, I had to have my natural lenses removed and have been wearing contacts ever since. Despite my disability, I've learned to find the opportunities in life. I've fought hard to stay as independent as possible even as I've asked for help. I memorize bus routes, look up restaurant menus ahead of time, and speak up in meetings and classes. Most of all, I learned to accept my life as it is.

But when I became a mother, a new, anxiety-induced haze settled over me. In the morning, the blurry shadows seemed more sinister, things to trip over and get tangled up in. I worried about my ability to care for my children. I stressed about not being able to read to them, to drive them, to see thermometers or slivers, diagnose strep throat or rashes. I worried about being a burden on my husband.

The only thing I *didn't* worry about was having to do it alone. And then, one day, my husband told me he was leaving.

The reality of being a solo mom introduced a whole new set of complications to my already complicated life. I wanted my kids to have a "normal" life but had no idea how to pull it all off, with them at different schools, me with a full-time job—and I don't drive! Those early days of parenting solo were crippling. When I took my contacts out at night, the only thing between me and near blindness was a pair of thick trifocal glasses. I worried that if something happened in the night—a fire, an intruder—I would be incapable of taking care of my kids, though my glasses were right there. I lay awake with my eyes trained on the lighted hallway, my thoughts a perfect storm of worry and fear and doubt.

Could I really do this alone?

Fearful that someone would try to take my kids away from me if I couldn't cope, I felt pressured to prove myself every day, to find work-arounds, and to persist despite my limitations. One day my son slipped and fell at a friend's house, resulting in a pretty bad concussion. Trying to keep him awake while waiting for a ride to the hospital was almost unbearable. But like so many other predicaments, we got through it.

As we all know, when you're a solo mom, there is no *try*: it's do or do not. School happens. Work happens. Doctor's appointments happen. I learned to let go of the impossible and use the resources I had. My mother came over every morning before work to help me get the kids to school. We put a secondhand swing set in the backyard so we could play at home when we couldn't make it to the park. During the years after my husband left, we survived. No, more than that: we thrived, trying new things and making new memories, like seeing my son earn belts in tae kwon do, teaching my daughter to read, and all the while earning my master's degree.

Through it all, we benefited from the tenderness and strength of all those who loved us and even those who didn't really know us. More than once, my neighbor showed up with a pot of homemade chicken soup because someone in my house was sick. When my mother called to tell me that my grandma had passed away and asked me to come over, I called a friend. Before I knew it, she was at my house with her half-folded laundry in a basket and a promise to stay as long as I needed her. My father came to get me, and I was able to spend time with my grieving family without worrying about traumatizing my children.

Our failures were tempered by triumphs, our lows softened by our highs. It wasn't easy, but it never felt insurmountable because I was enfolded in the loving arms of my community. I know there will never be a day in my life when I don't think of all the family, friends, colleagues, and even strangers who lent a hand or a shoulder, and smile knowing that I—that we—are loved.

Being a single mother was the right thing for me. But I have tremendous help from my friends. They're in love with my kids, and my kids are in love with them.

—Edie Falco

XIII

from *Twenty-One Love Poems*

—————

Adrienne Rich

The rules break like a thermometer,
quicksilver spills across the charted systems,
we're out in a country that has no language
no laws, we're chasing the raven and the wren
through gorges unexplored since dawn
whatever we do together is pure invention
the maps they gave us were out of date
by years . . . we're driving through the desert
wondering if the water will hold out
the hallucinations turn to simple villages
the music on the radio comes clear—
neither *Rosenkavalier* nor *Götterdämmerung*
but a woman's voice singing old songs
with new words, with a quiet bass, a flute
plucked and fingered by women outside the law.

Tahlequah

Isa Down

Tahlequah's baby lived for half an hour. Although it's not unusual for some mammals to carry their lost babies with them, Tahlequah carried her baby on a mourning tour for an unprecedented seventeen days and one thousand miles in oil-laden waters, devoid of enough fish to feed the pod, let alone a grieving mother whale. She labored to push the weight of her baby against currents, diving deep, lifting her above the choppy waves, up toward the sky and light and air.

Exhausted and hungry, Tahlequah carried on. Members of the pod stepped in to help carry her baby, allowing Tahlequah time to recharge, ensuring the continuity of the family unit. In a very real sense they were allowing her to rest, to breathe, while they carried her sorrow across the sea. A mourning mother, supported by the women around her. And for a few strong mothers, our pods keep us afloat, too, lifting us to the surface, taking deep breaths, and pushing forward.

In those few, brief moments, we float uninhibited, weightless, breathing deep. Until, suspended, we forge forward, a little lighter.

All the Single Ladies

Jennifer Baumgardner

The summer of 2007, when my son Skuli was almost three, I flew back early from a trip to Fargo so I could attend a party for Jenny and Sara Jane, two friends of mine who were celebrating their five-year relationship. Jenny and Sara Jane were a decade younger than I, Smith graduates with great style and even more beautiful politics. I was excited to go to their ceremony, which struck me as risky and brave. Their families weren't always comfortable and on board with their daughters' sexuality. Having everyone convene for this celebration of a gay relationship was, to my mind, a big deal. I was hungry for examples of alternative family-making, having logged nearly three years as a single mom by choice.

I was used to traveling alone, but that didn't make it any more pleasant when things went awry. Skuli was easy, but it wasn't like I had another adult to carry the bags, figure out the missed connection, or help clean up the milk vomit after the bumpy flight—things which happened with annoying regularity. It was a blazing hot July afternoon when we arrived at JFK after a long flight. I threw our bags in

Skuli's Sit 'n' Stroll, a car seat/stroller combo that I used in airports like a wheelbarrow when I traveled with him. Carrying him on one hip, I slogged out to the long-term parking lot. Our car, a 17-year-old red Honda Civic, shimmered in the heat. This isn't good, I thought, heart sinking, because one of the many quirks of this vehicle (passed down from mother to sister to me) was that it wouldn't start when parked in direct sunlight. I fastened Skuli's car seat into the cauldron of the backseat and turned the ignition, praying it would turn over. Nothing. I waited two minutes. Still nothing. Again—

"We should call someone to help us," Skuli offered from his microwave oven perch. He was good at intuiting our next step.

I called someone (JFK Roadside Assistance, maybe?) and soon a young guy arrived to jump our battery. "It's not the battery," I said, wishing I had thought to pack snacks and a water bottle for Skuli. "This car doesn't start in heat. I have to wait until sundown."

"It's the battery, Ma'am," the car guy said. After ten more minutes of needless jumping, hope, and disappointment, he offered to drive us in his tow truck to the nearest garage. Feeling a familiar financial panic, I mentally calculated the cost of this crisis—$60 for tow, $50 for car service home, God knows how much to "fix" the car (i.e., let car come to room temperature)—and wondered if witnessing Jenny and Sara Jane's commitment was worth the expense. I decided it was. We got home in time for me to shower and change, drop Skuli at his dad's for the night, and head to the party.

On a Brooklyn rooftop that night, drinking restoratively, I met Sara Jane's mom. A former nurse with great bone structure, frosted blonde hair, and a mini dress, her whole body vibed, "Be surprised that I have two adult daughters." She was a former single mother, and as we continued to drink and listen to the iPod playlist Jenny and Sara Jane had selected for this night, she prodded me for stories about my life. After each story, she'd shake her head and say, "Be selfish, Jen. You've got to be selfish."

I was used to getting unsolicited advice about my life, especially from people I considered to be less than knowledgeable. Some of it I gratefully accepted, like the offers to come over for Sunday dinner, and the used baby equipment my friends were always finding for me. Sometimes, though, I sensed not so much helpfulness but pity. I mean, I felt bad for some of them, what with their unhappy marriages and wilting sex lives, but I got the feeling that they used me to feel better about their own lives. "I know it must be so hard," these friends would say, flattening me into a stereotype with their sympathy faces (furrowed brow, lips pressed into a droopy frown) and their "Does Skuli have male role models? Is his dad, you know, involved?" concerns.

The truth is, it was hard. I woke up in the middle of the night worried about bills, anxious that I'd have coverage for Skuli while I was working. I brought him to parties with me not because he loved hanging out at adults' houses at 11:30 p.m., but because it was that or never socialize. But . . . I was happy. I'd never felt so much love and independence at once.

Back at the party, I attempted to respond to Sara Jane's mom. As a single mother, I was not selfish—that suffix "ish" connoting something gross or halfway. It's more like I was self-full. It was definitely a time in my life in which I had to rely on myself more than ever before, and yet my life was very rich with other people: Christine dropping by on the way home from work because I've conveyed that friends are always welcome, saying yes to spontaneous invitations to the Bronx Zoo because Skuli and I don't have to negotiate anyone else's schedule, New Year's Eves with Amy and Peter, sleepovers at Gillian's because we only need one bed.

The nuclear family, I noted, was a more closed home, electrons orbiting around the nucleus of the dinner table, ordered primarily by the schedules of its members. In my single-lady status, my home was open. I controlled the doors, and I wanted people to come in. My friends and family showed up for me all of the time. My sister Jessica, happily married and also a mother, marveled at how much help from friends and family I marshaled. "I guess I'm not afraid to ask," I said, attempting to analyze the discrepancy. "And people assume I need it, of course, which is kind of humiliating."

"Not as humiliating as needing it even though you have a partner," Jessica responded.

Clearly, Jessica wasn't one of the condescending types, but I gravitated toward single parent friends after Skuli was born. We were the ones who always dropped our kids late at school and got stern, condescending looks from the teachers. We brought our children to cocktail parties and readings, because it was that or we couldn't go. The single moms had scuffed shoes; our roots grown out from a little too much time between hair appointments. Superficially, we were more bedraggled, but we were also a really sturdy, actualized crew. Alan (as a man, an honorary single mom) was a poet, professor, and art critic who kept a perfect house for himself and Sophie. Sixty-something Merle owned the largest abortion clinic in the country and became a self-made millionaire before adopting Sasha from Siberia. Liliana had left Poland, escaped her abusive husband, and was raising Anna and Alex while working full time and going back to school. Sally wanted the baby but not the bad-boy baby daddy, and was raising her son exactly how she wanted—with organic food, no sugar, and lots of travel. Lorraine had three children, two exes, three enormously successful salons, and, in spite of being dyslexic, had written a book. We shared a common currency—the bracing combination of independence and terror. The independence was precious—"I get to write three nights a week," as Alan would often say—but it was the terror (Food on table! Clothes on kid! Insurance! Tuition!) that kept us motivated.

I felt lonely some days—the obvious ones, like Valentine's Day and Mother's Day—but the other days I felt this magical self-reliance. "Trust thyself," as Emerson wrote, "every heart vibrates to that iron string." I had ample opportunity to learn to trust myself, and maybe opportunity (also known as necessity) is just what one needs. Single parenthood was good for me, but people tend to feel bad for the children of single mothers, too, I noted. The assumption was that boys needed a role model and girls needed to know their dad would love and protect them. Heading into the subway one day, I was struggling with the stroller (Skuli in it and heavy) and my bags. Out of the corner of my eye, I saw a teen thug walking toward me with a menacingly blank look on his face and his pants drooped. He leaned over, picked up my carriage, and, without a word, carried Skuli down the two flights of stairs to the subway platform. I sputtered a thank you. He looked me in the eye and said in a soft voice, "I was raised by a single mom, Ma'am."

My friend Amy was raised by a single mom. When she turned thirty, her friends made a book for her, each of us taking a page to extol her work ethic, dance ability, and generosity. Her mother's page had a snapshot of the two of them, taken when Amy was about five and her mother was in her young twenties. The photographer was behind the two. Her mother is pointing at a flower right in front of them, showing it to Amy. And Amy is pointing up and away, to something that her mom can't even see. She wrote that it wasn't the most flattering photo of the two of them, but it was a good example of their relationship. The caption Amy's mother wrote was "We make a good team. We make a good team."

The fact that she wrote it twice slayed me, but I was most struck by seeing my tough, confident, sunny friend cry as she read the words. I think Amy knew that thing that I know and that Skuli knows and that all of the single moms know: the joy, beauty, and hard-earned satisfaction of being a good team. Days before that awful moment at JFK when my car wouldn't start, we visited my cousins at their lake cabin in Minnesota. Their house was crawling with kids and my cousin and her husband appeared to have an attractive, invitingly healthy relationship. The kids swam and hunted for minnows and played with toy cars. When it was time to leave, Skuli threw himself on the ground and cried, "No, I won't go! I belong here."

He had done the same thing a few weeks earlier at Amy's house, at which there was the same appealing constellation of happy and fun parents, cool toys, and siblings. Both times, I felt a chill course through me, because his response struck me as maybe true and certainly insightful. Not that he needed to have two parents, but there was something about the joviality and regularity of that home that either vibrated with what he knew about other people and missed in his own life—or it just felt right in some meaningful way that his three-year-old self needed to assert.

To me, it hurt, because I knew I belonged with him but I didn't belong there—and I wanted him to believe, as I did, that we were lucky that things had worked out as they did, that our lives were unique and wonderful. Was I just being selfish?

"Be selfish"—these words echoed in my brain the summer Skuli was three. What did it mean? Was it selfish to stay a unit of two, because Skuli would have to shoulder the burdens of my aging alone? Or was it selfish to have a love life when I had a young child who needed me? I could see it both ways and many more.

It may have just been a coincidence, but after that "selfish" conversation, I got my mojo back. By mojo, I mean my sexual self. I began dating again later that month, and within a few weeks I met the man that would become the father of my second child and, later, this same man—BD—became my husband. Skuli has thrived in our nuclear family, stricter and more constant than what he knew before. I wonder sometimes if he remembers our former way of being. Will he know to help a struggling mom with her stroller in ten years?

"We don't spend as much time together," Skuli told me one day, while walking home from school. We were holding hands and he had been telling me about his life in an alternate universe he calls Boneland. "You spend a lot of time with BD now."

I squeezed his hand.

"Remember when we were just the two of us," Skuli asked, "and we'd sleep together in the same bed?"

"I do remember," I said. "We made a good team, Skuli."

We made a good team.

Chapter Three: A Day in the Life

You make it work. You keep getting out of bed.
Sometimes it's just because there's a cup of coffee
downstairs.

—Michelle Williams

When a Car Wreck Collides with Picking Up the Kids

Melissa Stephenson

Last June a Ford F-250 rear-ended me, pushing my car into the hitch of a flatbed truck at the peak of a Friday-afternoon rush hour. I remember the sound of metal bending metal as the truck pulled free from the shiny black economy car my son had named Darth. Afterward my friends said things like, "I can't believe it . . . Thank God the kids weren't with you . . . Your first new car? Ten days off the lot? And your back hurts? What terrible luck, Mama." But the wreck is not what unhinged me. The other driver had good insurance and accepted liability on the spot. Even the mild neck and back pain wasn't the cause of my upset. I felt out of my body anyway, having just completed my longest run ever—twenty miles—in preparation for my first marathon.

What made my chin tremble right after the accident—my first in thirty-nine years, and a minor collision at that—was the realization that I had no one to pick up my kids.

My phone had only 10 percent battery life, my first four emergency contacts were all out of town, and I could not think of a single human able to do summer-camp and day-care pickup for me. My son had been missing me more than usual that week and made me pinkie promise over breakfast that I would get him a half hour early, at exactly 4:30. The wreck happened two miles from his camp, at 4:25.

We moved to this town (their father's hometown) three years ago, months before the divorce. Their dad calls and pays child support, but he lives states away, sees them a few times a year, and the only family we have here are a pair of his aunts who take the children to dinner and occasionally babysit. I am grateful as hell for that help, perhaps because I have so little of it. I've worked hard to make friends here, but most were on vacation the week of the wreck. The aunts, too. I couldn't stop myself from imagining what would happen to my children if I'd been seriously injured. How long would they wait at camp and day care before the directors contacted their father? What would their father do from hundreds of miles away? Exactly how scared would my kids be? And how would I parent with broken limbs through the long-lit days of a Montana summer?

As I waited with the two other drivers for the cops to arrive, I ran through the details I don't share about being a solo mom: how the kids were two and five when their father left (too young to work a smartphone), so I taught them to walk across the street to the convenience store and ask for help if "anything ever happened to Mama." How the girl, still in diapers, used to point to the giant map on the wall, and yell over and over, "Where my dada be?" and accept no answers. How my son developed a habit of crying each time he saw me during one of his father's visits, associating my presence with his dad's departure. How he befriended kids at playgrounds, followed them to their fathers, then tried to sit in the strange men's laps in spite of his shyness. How on a playdate one kid said, "I think your dad isn't coming back," and we never invited him over again. How the girl spent the fall she turned three crying in her sleep, me awake listening. How each December they stand by, shiny and useless as ornaments, saying, "Thanks, Mom, thanks," as I struggle to get the Christmas tree through the door. How there is no one to help them buy me presents on holidays, so they make them in secret after bedtime. How we spend those holidays alone, all the friends we call family busy spending time with their real families. How when their father last visited, my son smiled and said, "Now everyone at school will know my dad is real."

It takes seconds for the fear that fuels these moments to pass through me. The story it urges me to tell is far more damaging than the strain of running twenty miles or the impact of the wreck. On my last bit of battery power, a text from a single dad friend rolls in, and I realize his son is at camp with mine, my daughter is at the daycare where our boys met, and we're saved. He gets them in minutes. I make it home first and call in pizza delivery. The girl and boy tumble into my arms, a week's worth of artwork stuffed into their backpacks. They pause to inspect the smashed ends of the car, impressed. The news about pizza distracts them—a rare treat—and the story shifts so swiftly from *What if?* to *Enough.* Because it seems no accident, finally, that we always have enough. The three of us snuggle in bed that night, watching a movie together as the sun sets, too rich in luck and goodness to think about my aching neck, elevated legs, or the stray popcorn leaving love crumbs between the sheets.

How to Comfort a
Small Child

Abby Murray

a collage of found advice for parenting through deployment

Wallpaper the living room
with a world map.
Put a green thumbtack
through Fort Carson,
a red tack through Kandahar.
Buy stuffed bears
dressed in camouflage and dog tags,
sew a recording of dad's voice
into the bear's chest
where its heart would be.
Have him read stories

or recite prayers.
Spell out certain words
on the phone: d-e-a-d,
m-i-s-s-i-n-g, w-o-u-n-d-e-d.
Be organized. Make lists.
Children want to see order,
they need to see you sad
but not too sad.
Keep busy. Keep a journal.
Sing songs. Sleep well.
Make daddy dolls
and daddy pillows.
If it is economically feasible,
print a life-size cutout
of dad with arms spread wide.
Children can hug cutouts
and photographs.
Try yoga. Try karate.
Build memory boxes
and fill them with sentimental items,
an old watch or clean t-shirt.
Build picture frames.
Build scrapbooks.
Projects that require building
give children a sense of purpose.
Limit the family's exposure
to news programs.
Expect children to ask
about torture and ransom,
topics beyond their years.
Use words they understand.
Express love. Try fun outings:

days at the zoo
and movies in the park.
Be joyful. Don't dwell.
Read articles written for moms.
Avoid taking on added responsibilities
such as job promotions,
transfers or school programs.
Try cocoa, try jelly beans, try gum.
Write brief letters.
Ask the Red Cross.
Ask your doctor.
Ask to speak with the principal.
Make friends
with women who understand,
women with children
and spouses who haven't called in days.
When your daughter
flushes her plastic fox
down the toilet
and says he went to Afghanistan,
don't read into it.
Call a plumber.

Rules for Being Twenty

Ariel Gore

My women's lit professor says I own the language. I can make new words and new stories if the old ones don't suit me. It's how we keep the language alive, she says. I like the way her tongue crests her upper lip when she says alive. Alive and thriving.

Don't watch her tongue, Ariel. Just look down. Pretend you think the baby woke up. Pretend you're taking notes.

Tongue to lip.

"Read these," she says, and she pushes two paperbacks across her desk: *Silences* by Tillie Olsen and *Sister Outsider* by Audre Lorde.

Rules for being twenty:
Keep the language alive.
Keep the baby athrive.
Don't let your brain get sucked into the strip mall of suburban
    motherhood.

If there are only two options, always choose material poverty over
   psychic poverty.
If there are only two options, create a third option as soon as possible.

The Sonoma County welfare office was an option.

   I let the baby play with the bright plastic rings on the cold
linoleum floor as I filled out paperwork. I lied here and there on the
paperwork. I didn't lie, too. But I always felt like I was lying.

   No, I don't get anything beyond tuition in student loan money.

   *I don't get one hundred dollars a month from my Gammie
Evelyn—red envelopes that smell like Paloma Picasso perfume.*

   No, I don't know where my baby's father lives.

   *Yes, I have the documentation to prove it: This address on this
fake lease. This copy of a check. This state-issued ID. Please just give us
our check.*

Under the fluorescent lights, women studied their pre-law books.
They threatened to slap their crying children. Women checked their
watches, their beepers. They chewed blue bubblegum. They filled out
paperwork.

   Outside, men waited in cars.

   I read *Silences* by Tillie Olsen.

   A social worker yelled at the mother two spots ahead of me in
line. "You lied," she said, and she leaned across the counter, pointed
a long, curved fingernail at the woman.

   I listened, but I couldn't figure out what lie the lying woman
had been caught telling.

   Maybe she secretly got one hundred dollars a month from her
Gammie Evelyn, too.

   Maybe there was a man waiting for her in a car outside.

   The social worker flashed a silver tooth. "Why did you lie?"

The lying woman adjusted her baby's position on her hip, pulled an older child standing next to her close. "I lied to get the food stamps."

My heart swelled at the honesty of that. *I lied to get the food stamps.*

The social worker squinted and shook her head. "You would lie to get food stamps?"

A woman behind me sucked her teeth. "Like '*Thou shall not lie*' is one of the goddamn Ten Commandments?"

The lying woman shrugged at the social worker. "Listen, lady," she said, and she pointed her index finger right back at her. "You'd lie to get food stamps too. If your kids were hungry, you know you'd lie."

The social worker shook her head like she didn't know.

She'd lie.

The mother walked away, shaking her head. She put her baby down and let her play with the bright plastic rings on the cold linoleum floor, and she redid her paperwork to get back in line.

There were other lies we would learn to tell.

The woman in front of me scurried up to the counter, but just then her toddler started crying loud and she spoke softly and the social worker snapped, "I can't hear you over your kid's tantrum. Back of the line."

I whispered quick in Maia's ear, "We have to be perfect." And we stepped forward.

Evening Guilt

Kristie Robin Johnson

I should be proud of the calm
in his 10-year-old voice saying

he's fine, finished his homework,
parroting *I love you* before he hangs up.

But I am mostly bitter
in this sweet moment

because he is alone, swallowed
into a silent, sunless house,

taking care of himself
(an unnatural task for a child)

slicing his own apple, pouring
his own cereal into a Spiderman

bowl, washing his own dishes.
Closing the door behind him

and locking himself in, being
his own armor, protection, and peace

while I make do, 80 miles away
in a town he can't fathom.

On the ride home, I pray
aloud that these lonely

dusk hours will not be
his single remembrance

of me. I pray that he
recalls the smell of pink

grapefruit after kissing
my freshly cleaned face

goodnight. I ask God to
only let him conjure up

autumn Saturday mornings,
our breath forming small clouds

between us as I snap his
chinstrap, tighten the laces on
his cleats, and send him off

to battle. Let his reminiscing
be filled with the laughter and

reverie of singing along to
Bruno Mars as he stirs the pasta

and I brown the sausage
for Sunday dinner. Let the

small, kind moments swell
in his heart, leave no room

for dejected sunsets, bruised
promises still needing to heal.

I'm the Woman Who Hit Your Daughter with My Car

Courtney Christine

Sometimes I play a little game with myself while I'm driving. When I have a general idea of where I need to go, I turn off the GPS. I feel my way there instead. It's kind of like finding the bathroom in the dark by running your hands along the wall. You have to slow down and focus on each step.

I was driving without my GPS the night I hit a little girl with my car.

The next morning, my two elementary school–aged daughters took one look at my face and knew something was wrong. I don't like to worry them if I can avoid it. But the puffiness around my eyes—evidence of a long night of crying—gave me away.

I'd had a lot of practice hiding things from my daughters. Over the last year, I'd kept quiet about the main details of my divorce from their father. My girls didn't know why we had spent so many nights sleeping in other people's houses or why I was able to obtain a divorce so quickly. For years, the explosive fights and put-downs had been muffled, because I had learned at what point in the conversation a door needed to be closed or a fan turned on. They didn't know I'd become skilled in various anger de-escalation techniques.

They didn't know how fear had slowly, over years, seeped into my bones, turning me into someone who jumped too quickly when someone walked up behind me. They just thought that was one of Mom's endearing quirks. They even teased me about it.

All that hiding I did was strategic: I wanted to save my daughters from pain. I didn't want their happy childhood memories of a mom and dad who'd loved each other to be tainted. I didn't want them to think poorly of their father, someone they loved and wanted a relationship with.

My daughters knew the basic facts: Their dad had been sick and had made poor choices. They also knew that people are supposed to forgive other people when they say they're sorry. And they knew their dad had said sorry plenty of times.

They knew their mother had left anyway.

Understandably, they were angry with me. It was a quiet kind of anger, simmering right under the surface. It bubbled up whenever I made a ponytail too high, or when I sounded a little too happy talking to a friend, or when I was a few minutes late picking them up from camp. They didn't trust that I was paying attention. They didn't know if I was suffering as much as they were. Could I be trusted to keep my promises to them when I hadn't kept the vows of marriage to their dad?

Would I leave them, too?

In addition to feeling angry, they felt confused. We had once been a happy family of four. Our split was a surprise, an unexpected twist in the story, a car wreck on the way home from a trip to the park. And the person in the driver's seat was their mother.

"Why have you been crying?" they asked when they walked into the kitchen. I poured milk in cereal bowls and soaked a warm washcloth for my face.

I told them how I'd been driving down a one-way street lined with cars on my way to a friend's house. How I'd been approaching a stop sign, slowing to stop. That was when I'd felt a bump. And heard a scream.

A child's scream.

By the time I jumped out, a man was already scooping his daughter's body out of the road, an older girl running behind him. There was so much screaming—the man, the little girl in his arms, the girl at his heels. Me.

Someone dialed 911. Others crowded around. "You have to lay her flat on the ground!" I shouted over all the voices. She was conscious, and the only visible injury was a cut above her eyebrow—both good signs. But I knew from a first aid class that lying flat might prevent her from further injury if her spine was broken or she was bleeding internally. Sometimes everything can look fine from the outside, but on the inside, it's all falling apart.

Eventually the little girl stopped flailing, and the screaming subsided. Someone alerted the girl's mother, who rushed over from the apartment building across the street. She wore long, blue scarves and used the hem of her skirt to blot blood and tears from her daughter's face. Her movements wafted the smell of cooking spices. Though she exuded calm, I detected fear in her furrowed brow.

I know that look.

The family spoke with an accent. The father had what appeared to be tribal scars across his face. I later learned that this family had recently emigrated from Nigeria, eager for a new and better life. The father had been playing with his children at the park, and when it was time to go inside for dinner, five-year-old Adeena had rushed across the middle of the street without looking first. She'd run head down, not a care in the world, the way young children do when they have no reason to fear something bad could ever happen to them.

As the ambulance siren grew closer, I stepped away from that scene—a mother, father, and big sister crouching around the body of their baby. There was nothing more I could do. The knowledge of what I'd already done thickened in my chest. I didn't want them to see me cry. I backed away, walked to the end of the block, and buried my face in my hands.

Someone's happy hope of a new life had been shattered. Because of me.

Two small, warm arms wrapped themselves around my waist. I turned to find Adeena's older sister looking up at me, her brown eyes moist under a sequined hijab.

"Don't cry, lady," she soothed in the same voice I use when my daughters scrape their knees on the sidewalk. "Don't you cry. She will be OK. We will be OK."

I didn't know for sure that Adeena would be OK. After all, I had *felt* her, not seen her, from inside my car. I was too old and experienced to wish for such good luck. But for a moment, I put all that away. I held Adeena's sister, no older than ten or eleven, and she held me.

The paramedics wheeled Adeena into the back of the ambulance. Her mother went with her. Her father and sister went home, and the police said I could go home, too. I wasn't found to be at fault for the accident. I hadn't been speeding; my eyes had been on the road. It was just one of those awful things that happens. Sometimes there is no one to blame.

I didn't sleep that night. I hadn't thought to ask for Adeena's family's phone number so that I could check on her. All the area hospitals told me the same thing—they couldn't give out patient information even if I knew the child's name. I spent hours reading about internal injuries after car accidents. I wondered if the cut on Adeena's forehead meant that her head had been hit hard. I worried about brain damage. Or worse.

After breakfast I tracked down the official accident report, which included a phone number for Adeena's family. Her mother answered.

"I'm so sorry to call you this early. I'm the woman who hit your daughter with my car. I wanted to know if she's OK."

I learned that the bump I'd felt from my car was the side-view mirror impacting Adeena's face. I also learned that no other part of her body had been hit. She didn't even have a concussion. She was bruised and traumatized—but she was going to be OK.

That afternoon, my daughters and I made a Target run. We ran up and down the toy aisles, yelling, "I bet she'd like this!" and "Let's get her this one!" We settled on a baby doll with thick curly hair and a set of bristle blocks for Adeena. For her older sister, we picked out a mega-sized Lego set and a craft kit. The biggest box of ice cream drumsticks, a giant pack of sidewalk chalk, and a gift card all went into the cart.

"Wow, Mom." My eleven-year-old noted the stuffed cart and my unusually jovial spirit. "It's like Christmas in here."

She was right. I receive SNAP benefits and round out the rest of our grocery budget at food pantries. I don't shop like this. Not even on Christmas.

"This is a special day," I explained. "Maybe you want to pick out something, too?" Her eyes brightened. The girls tossed in some gum and more sidewalk chalk.

I wasn't sure what kind of greeting I would get from Adeena's family. I would have been fine with dropping off our Target bags at the door. But when I called them, Adeena's family buzzed us up.

At the top of the landing stood Adeena's father. I noted the scars on his face, his muscular arms, the breadth of his chest. A huge man.

His smile was huge, too. He spread his arms wide to gather me in. "I'm so glad you came," he said, as his family stepped out from behind him. "We were so worried about you."

After introductions, my daughters pulled each toy out one by one and ceremoniously handed them over to the appropriate child. At one point, Adeena's parents playfully nudged her in my direction. Her wounds were already beginning to scab over, dark teardrops above her right eyebrow.

I remembered something about the accident just then—something I'd completely forgotten I'd done in a state of shock. When Adeena's father rushed her to the side of the road, I'd made an attempt to grab her from his arms. It was the impulse of a mother to pull her children to her chest when they've run to her, hurt. I had backed off when I realized this was not my child to comfort.

"May I give you a hug?" I asked Adeena. Her parents nodded. She shrugged and let me.

As we drove away, the girls and I replayed the events at Adeena's home. We talked about how good it felt to know their family's nightmare had not turned tragic. How things could have been worse. How lucky they were.

How lucky we were.

At the next red light, I adjusted the rearview mirror. My younger daughter was cradling her sidewalk chalk and chomping through her pack of gum. My older daughter's eyes were focused on something just beyond the window. The perpetual knot in her eyebrows had relaxed. Her hands were lying flat on her knees, instead of popping her knuckles in the nervous habit she'd picked up recently.

It was as if, for a moment at least, she had found her way to something she needed in the darkness.

I turned back to the road. The light turned green.

You don't have the bad cop when you're the good cop, and when you're the good cop you don't have the bad cop; you're like the whole police force in your family.

—Katie Couric

Life after the NICU

Sarah Netter

I got the call in the middle of the night: my baby was being delivered eleven weeks ahead of schedule, by emergency Cesarean section. I was nearly paralyzed with fear. For nearly three months, from New York, I had been in touch via email and phone with his birth mother, who lived in rural Mississippi. I had marveled at every sonogram she sent me. I had teared up when I heard his heartbeat for the first time. I had scheduled to fly down to Mississippi for another ultrasound in a few weeks. I had assumed I had time left, months even, to prepare to become a mother.

Instead, this phone call: his birth mother's life was in danger; doctors at a nearby hospital were delivering him to save them both.

I booked a ticket on the earliest plane—5:55 a.m.

Two years earlier, when I decided to join the growing ranks of single mothers by choice, I knew adoption was an often-bumpy path—and I worried about every possible bump. Having a two-pound, eight-ounce preemie wasn't one of them.

But there we were: me, the impossibly tiny and critically ill infant, and his birth mother, who had just been through one of the most terrifying and heartbreaking ordeals of her life.

My son's seventy-three days in the NICU brought swells of love and pure joy, sheer drops into terror, and seemingly inhuman levels of anxiety. I watched my precious child's oxygen levels dip dangerously low while a nurse hand-pumped air into his limp body. I celebrated clear lung X-rays, only to be devastated two days later by sacs so full of fluid they appeared solid white. I cheered as he learned to suck from a bottle, only to slump my shoulders in defeat when his respiratory system couldn't handle eating and breathing at the same time. I heard his monitors' clanging alarms even in my sleep—when I was fortunate enough to get any sleep. Then Discharge Day came, flooding all those emotions through me at the same time.

Not wanting to jinx my son's prospects by buying baby gear too early, I had nothing. Now I blew through Target at warp speed, grabbing anything that looked remotely useful, including a first aid kit that was laughable considering the medical equipment that would accompany my son home.

I hauled the car seat, still wrapped in plastic, into the NICU and buckled in my son. Tipping the scales at more than six pounds, his cheeks were rosy, and he was learning to smile at me—the picture of a healthy baby. The thought of bringing him home had me literally quivering with excitement—and fear. How would I parent this baby without the monitor screens and vitals checks that assured me he was, in fact, healthy? I had become a good NICU mom, but what kind of mom would I be outside those sterile walls?

I was about to find out. I signed the required paperwork, received a receipt (yes, I got an actual piece of paper that read "Receipt of Infant"), and with a grand send-off including flowers, sweets, and hugs from the team of doctors and nurses who had taken care of both of us for two-and-a-half months, we left the hospital.

One of my son's NICU nurse practitioners, Andrea, helped us get to the extended-stay hotel where my son and I would start our life together, until the courts issued travel paperwork for us to go home. The baby was sound asleep when Andrea left, still strapped into his car seat on the hotel room floor. I sat nearby, staring at him, willing him not to wake up until I figured out what I was supposed to do next.

Even though he was nearly three months old by then, he was the size of a newborn fresh from the womb, beautifully perfect. He showed no hint of what he'd been through, except that he had come "home" with a monitor that would sound an alarm if his heart or respiratory rate fell dangerously low, a bad habit he hadn't quite kicked yet. I checked and rechecked the monitor. Was it attached to the right part of his chest? Was it too tight? Not tight enough?

I paced around the hotel room like a woman caught in a cage. But in a cage is exactly where I wanted to be. In a cage, I could protect him.

I hadn't slept more than a few hours over the last three days, and I figured my son would be exhausted from his first day outside the NICU walls. So as the sun set, I changed him into his onesie, gave him a fresh diaper, and fed him. We cooed at each other the entire time. This, I thought, is what motherhood was meant to be. He looked at me as if I knew what to do. I checked and rechecked the monitor. And then I laid him down.

He slept for an hour and a half right off the bat, but the rest of the night would be cut up in thirty-minute intervals of trial and error—turning on the ceiling fan to prevent SIDS, turning on the heater to compensate for the wind tunnel created by the ceiling fan, preparing bottles of formula, spilling bottles of formula, attempting new sleep positions, and playing endless rounds of "find the paci, lose the paci." At 7:00 a.m., he finally fell asleep in my lap.

The next twelve hours were a blur. A rotation of NICU nurses stopped by the hotel every few hours. They brought food and hugs and gifts and helped with laundry. One babysat while I tried to nap, but I just tossed and turned, worrying. How would I ever figure out this parenting thing?

My son was fine; I was a wreck.

Andrea insisted on staying with me that night, leaving her own family to fend for themselves, so I could get some rest. Once a preemie mom herself, she knew what I didn't: six glorious hours of sleep could be a game-changer. The next day, bolstered by both a good REM cycle and a new perspective, I got it together.

I hadn't counted on how difficult it would be for my son to adjust to life outside the hospital. For the first two and a half months of his life, his nights had been filled with weight checks, blood draws, and the bright lights and alarms that are part of the scenery of the NICU. He had never slept in a dark, quiet room. He'd also grown accustomed to his incubator, his own little tiny apartment, where he was swaddled, safe, and often laid on his tummy to help him breathe easier. That had made sense in the NICU, but in real life, he had to learn to sleep on his back. Over the next few days, my son and I figured out our own rhythm and easily fell into it. The NICU nurses continued to visit us, but as friends, not caretakers.

Emboldened by my newfound ability to get us both through the night, I began taking him for walks around the hotel complex, the sun spilling across his face for the first time in his life. Then I got braver, taking him for a drive. It was only two miles down the road for a soup and salad from Wendy's, but I was so proud of both of us.

On these outings, my son's eyes would dart around, taking in each new sight, and then he would focus on me, the one constant in his short life. And he'd smile.

After ten days in the hotel, we got legal clearance to head home to New York. As time passed, I continued to shed my fear and anxiety, and I came to enjoy him for who he was: a happy, healthy baby boy. My son.

My Life as a Refugee

Faleeha Hassan

Translated by William M. Hutchins

Once my name appeared on a death list published in newspapers and on websites, I fled Iraq for the Turkish city of Eskişehir. After a month, I moved to Afyonkarahisar, where rent was more reasonable. But this mountain town had harsh winters. By 3:00 p.m., the temperatures descended below zero degrees, so cold that vendors' fruits and vegetables would freeze in the open-air markets.

During my time in Turkey, I did not meet a single Turk who spoke English or Arabic, but I did meet an Iraqi child who spoke fluent Turkish. I hired her for a modest fee to interpret for us whenever we went to a government bureau. Even with that help, it was not easy to enroll my children in school. The principal refused to admit them because they did not know Turkish. So I appealed to the superintendent of education. When he asked why I wanted to send my children to school, I replied, "To keep them warm!" He relented.

That was actually my reason for enrolling my children. At school they would be warm, unlike our apartment, which was unbearably cold. Though I had bought a coal-fired space heater, I was never able to get it to operate properly. Coal smoke would fill the entire apartment, so when I lit it, we almost suffocated. At night we wore wool socks, caps, leggings, and occasionally mittens, and we slept huddled together beneath four blankets.

The cold was not the only problem with the apartment. Our landlady was domineering. She had accused her own husband of theft and had him sent to prison. She had divided her house into four small apartments, and she lived in the best one with her teenage daughter and a huge dog she chained by the door. Each month, when I paid my rent, she would ask me for more money—a loan she would never repay. When I refused, she would become angry and speak so loudly that I could not understand her. As if that was not enough, she grabbed our lower water and electricity bills and left us her higher bills, insisting the lower bills were intended for her.

One morning my children and I woke to the sound of heavy pickaxes. When I opened the door, I was surprised to see three workmen outside. The landlady had hired them to demolish the steps to our residence. Infuriated, I contacted the police and phoned the child interpreter who explained my plight to the policemen. The landlord said new steps would be completed by the next morning. The police took no action. My children and I were confined to our quarters for three days. During those days I would write out a shopping list for an Iraqi neighbor, place it and some money in a basket, and lower it to her with a rope.

Speaking of shopping, on the mountain, the local open-air market was held on Sundays. Shopping was rather like climbing. One day, my foot slipped, and I fell a long way down the slope. People carried me home on a wooden stretcher. I could not get about for two weeks.

As I was healing, my son Ahmad caught German measles from a classmate. A doctor prescribed medication that cost 80 Turkish lira, about US$80 at the time—a horrific sum, compared to the cost of food and rent. Fresh fish, for example, might cost 5 lira, and the monthly rent for our apartment was only 250 lira. All the same, I had to purchase this medicine for my son, though that meant I lived on bread and water for a time. What else could I do?

Fearful, anxious, and lonely, my psychological condition was deteriorating. I had lost the ability to sleep at night. If I did fall asleep, I would wake a couple hours later, soaked with sweat, after nightmares about men trying to slay me or blow up the room around me. I asked the agency in charge of Iraqi refugees whether there was a psychiatrist who would treat me. A month later, an employee contacted me to tell me a Turkish woman psychiatrist could see me the next Friday at the bureau.

When the day came, I found the physician waiting for me with an Iraqi translator. She asked me some medical questions, and I told her candidly about my daily travails. She simply advised me to mix with other people, read the Qur'an, and wear a blue headscarf.

I wondered, "Has this physician ever treated a genuinely ill patient?" What could I do but thank her and leave?

I did follow the physician's suggestion to try to socialize. I started taking my children to a large public park. But when Turks caught sight of us, they would mock my children and me because our complexion was darker than theirs. So I would sit in a far corner of the park, away from the adults, watching the children play.

Eventually, my experiences and my insomnia motivated me to write a novella, *I Hate My City*. A friend offered to submit it to an Iraqi publishing house in Irbil, and the publisher agreed to print and distribute the novel. Three months later, I learned it had been released and would be displayed at an international fair in Irbil.

In my home country, I was known as "the Maya Angelou of Iraq."

My poetry books had angered political adversaries, which is why my children and I left. But I never felt comfortable in Turkey because it was not a safe distance from my enemies. So I started asking fellow Iraqis in Turkey about the possibility of leaving for a distant country. They told me that I needed to register with the UN in Ankara.

My children and I took a bus to Ankara. When we reached the UN office, we joined a crowd of people outside the door, waiting for entry. When we were finally admitted to a lobby, we joined another crowd from various parts of the globe.

Once we registered, a UN official asked why we were applying for humanitarian refugee status. I recounted my history of calamities. This was the first of three such interviews. Eventually, my children and I were assigned to America. We completed an admissions interview and attended a three-day workshop, which included physical exams to make sure we had no contagious or chronic diseases.

Because I had no family in America, representatives of a Catholic charity received us in New Jersey. Mrs. Cathy, the head of the organization, had secured an apartment for us in Gloucester, paying the rent in advance for three months. But some of our new neighbors were not ready to welcome Arab Muslims.

A woman who lived on the ground floor started harassing my children and me every day. She would turn up the volume of her TV and leave it like that all night long. At six in the morning, she would play the childish prank of ringing our doorbell. She would drop her husband's metal weights on the ground, making our whole apartment shake. After I discovered her taking photos of my children with her mobile phone, I became so frightened I complained to the apartment complex manager. The manager couldn't stop the harassment, so I contacted the police. My tormentor told the officer that her husband had been deployed to fight in Iraq and that since we were Iraqis we should be killed. The policeman merely smiled. I was obliged to move to another apartment, far away from her.

Even in my new home, it isn't easy being a Muslim woman who wears a headscarf in America. Many people, knowing nothing about my children and me, assume we are terrorists. All they know about Islam is the distorted picture some media outlets broadcast every day. I wish they could see we all share a common humanity; that's the important thing.

The Rookie

January Gill O'Neil

America under the lights
at Harry Ball Field. A fog rolls in
as the flag crinkles and drapes

around a metal pole.
My son reaches into the sky
to pull down a game-ender,

a bomb caught in his leather mitt.
He gives the ball a flat squeeze
then tosses it in from the outfield,

tugs his cap over a tussle of hair
before joining the team—
all high-fives and handshakes

as the Major boys line up
at home plate. They are learning
how to be good sports,

their dugout cheers interrupted only
by sunflower seed shells spat
along the first base line.

The coach prattles on
about the importance of stealing
bases and productive outs

while a teammate cracks a joke
about my son's 'fro, then says,
But you're not really black . . .

to which there's laughter,
to which he smiles but says nothing,
which says something about

what goes unsaid, what starts
with a harmless joke, routine
as a can of corn.

But this is little league.
This is where he learns
how to field a position,

how to play a bloop in the gap—
that impossible space where
he'll always play defense.

This Is Your Life

Fern Capella

This is your life when you're in a dream at 5 a.m. running fast with your arms empty, and you wake up to a screech and you think maybe you hopped a train, but then you feel something warm next to you in bed, and you remember

you had a baby three weeks ago.

And he's crying, so you reach over to soothe your precious baby and pull him up on top of you and as you do his diaper comes off and his poop is now all over you, so you summon the courage to stand up and clean up, so now you're naked as your parents walk through your room smiling, "Good morning," on their way to get coffee 'cause

you're twenty-one and single

and you're living in their living room. But not for long 'cause their next question is, "When do you think you'll be up to moving out?"

and you think, "When do I think I'll be up to moving my body?" but you smile bravely and say, "Probably by next week." So they leave so you can breathe, but breathing is for the baby who you remember again and check on 'cause

breath is such a fragile thing.

Then your stitches tug and you can't imagine any of this ending, but then you can't imagine any other beginning than the one of this amazing life you call your son, and the stupid "You Are My Sunshine" song that set you hysterically crying in front of your baby's pediatrician yesterday as you thought of the second part—when the sunshine is taken away—and you think, "How could I take that?" and you fully realize a mother's terror.

Those poor mothers everywhere.

But really you could sob all day, and who has time 'cause you're a mother now and your three-ton tits are the last place you have been attacked in this war against your body as you hold one in each hand to shower while you have head out/ass in to sing your baby ga-ga songs about maybe getting a fucking break from someone sometime.

Like his father, that slime.

And your mother hears you and is appalled and you are disgusted with yourself and swear his name will never be mentioned when your baby knows what you're saying even though it seems like he always has with the beautiful way he surveys you and your heart hits the floor.

You love him like sapphires under your tongue.

And who else but his father calls to say he remembers why he made your baby and he could love you if you let him make another one. And you think that even you didn't have anything to do but host the miracle that was being formed inside you and this asshole getting some ass one night most certainly did not either, so you thank him for his microscopic gift of one in ten billion sperm that happened to make the prettiest baby you've ever seen and hang up thinking,

It's mostly between you and God now.

And so you pull some energy out from somewhere deep 'cause you realize you won't be wanting any breaks from Him, and you get you and your baby dressed and make your way to the store and there, in the midst of checkout, you're roused from this seemingly endless daze to find the store clerk holding your whining baby with spit-up on his dark blue uniform and you writing a bad check with shaky fingers and the lady behind you in line dying to find out why your skin is whiter than white, like Tide with bleach, and your baby looks like a Cuban who has just been rescued from the seas, and you snarl and say, "You wanna see my stretch marks?" 'cause

he could only be your baby.

You get nauseous to think otherwise, though that seems to be a better option as your mother mentions later that, "It's never too late to consider adoption," and you tell her, "It's never too late to consider suicide," and it's all just so sugar sweet. If you could just melt for a moment with your baby and rest, you might just see clear but you're interrupted in your merging by a phone call from your very childless, gay best friend who wants to go out later with you and "it"—the baby—but he's nervous that everyone might think he's the father 'cause the poor kid doesn't have one and that's the curse of the single mother.

You're always left open for insult and somehow you're always tough enough to take it and

that's the blessing of the single mother.

It's not til much later that you have time to write these things and your back is tired and your bones are tired and even your pen seems tired, but the paper is your lover and you tell it everything and you tell it how you're terrified and how you're probably a terrible mother but only on the shitty days and you tell it how you've never imagined a love so consuming and close to God as you have for this tender life sleeping in a curl next to you and you doze off exhausted to wake an hour later, around 5 a.m.

to a screech.

I think it's really important for every mother to find their own way.

—Solange Knowles

Crying It Out

Robin Silbergleid

You never knew how much you could crave it, crave anything. You crave it more than a woman who hasn't had sex in seven years, more than a three-year fertility patient after her sixth IVF, more than a crack addict looking to score. This is not a craving of a pickles-and-ice-cream variety, some pregnant woman on a TV commercial for Taco Bell who wants something chewy and crunchy and cheesy all at once. Fuck chocolate cake. Fuck Dr. Sears and attachment parenting. Fuck the pediatrician who says *let him cry*. By the time your son is ten months old and you haven't slept more than two consecutive hours, you crave sleep so much you understand those women who put their babies in microwaves or overdose them on Benadryl. You literally aren't seeing straight—everything in front of you curves, and there is a flashing light in the corner of your right eye that hasn't gone away for days. Your hands are shaking, and you throw him in the stroller and push it over the hump in the kitchen floor and around the dining room, furious uncountable laps. And then you sit on the floor with him in your arms and you sob. You make potatoes and call your mother because mothers will do almost anything to help their children sleep. You think about all the Inuit words for snow and think about all the different kinds of sleep, kinds of fatigue, like different flavors of ice cream, all so marvelous you want each cool, sweet concoction, strawberry cheesecake, mint chocolate chip, rocky road. You're so desperate you'd probably settle for a Tofutti rice dreamsicle or sugar-free vanilla. You crave them all: the one that hits you in the chest when you're coming down with a cold, the progesterone-woozy drag through early pregnancy, the blur in your eyes when you've been awake since three in the morning and you're finally ready to nod off. When the young resident gives you the depression inventory and diagnoses you with *mild insomnia*, you try very hard not to laugh in his face. You drink wine, you take a couple of Ambien, you put your son to your breast. The rocking chair moves back and forth in the moonlight, toward the calling dawn. Milk drips down his chin, *fleur de sel* and caramel. It has never tasted so sweet.

They Give Awards for That

Lee Nash

They're giving out prizes to single moms.
Finally some appreciation.
I wrote my application
and drew in my own boxes
because there wasn't one
for sleeping in the corridor so your children
can each have a room.
Or for living opposite the seedy bar
and running the gauntlet outside your front door.
There was one for taking care of their health
and I added podiatrist, optician, cardiologist, and dermatologist
to "general."
I wrote four years, eight months,
and zero
in "contact with father"
and "alimony."

I scored 10 for mental anxiety
and 10 for chronic despair.
Obama and Clinton wrote references,
and praised their own moms in turn.
I'm in with a chance to win.
When they photograph me with my medal
like a true Olympian,
I'm going to bite on it.
With any luck it won't crack.

Chapter Four:
Good Morning Heartache

You always have to carry on. And you can because you have to.

—Kate Winslet

Why We Stay

VersAnnette Blackman-Bosia

We stay because we are tired
We stay because we are forlorn
We stay because we have been
abandoned
rejected
left to figure it out on our own
as girls
saw Daddy do it to Mama
and Mama do it to Daddy
and Daddy do it to brother
and brother do it to his girl
and his girl take it
and his girl screams
and his girl fight back
but she always come back
We stay because we think we have it

under control because the soul bleeds
and we cry out Jesus as Band-Aids
We stay because we are tired of trying
fighting to change a trajectory
etched in our veins
We stay because we hear the song of
shame-filled ignorance
claiming that we feign innocence
We stay because violence is a code
a practice, a belief
a mutual love language
and that language is empowered by silence
and silence only exists when the throat chakra is closed
and hope floats
We stay because we are lost
We stay because we don't see a tomorrow
We stay because sorrow outweighs joy
We stay because we are tired
We stay because we were taught
not to give up
on love on him on God on us on the black man, the family, the kids
though we are consistently quitting on ourselves
We stay because we've got nothing else to lose
We stay because our spirits are broken
and we are choking on self-hate
We stay because we are afraid to speak up
to incriminate to let go to fess up to truths
too painful to acknowledge
and everyone thinks we like it
We stay because we've been tired since way back when
We stay because being taken and beaten has always been our
    reel, against our will

and leaves us
floating on the edge of defeat
somewhere zipped inside torture and reality
an undefined space
an unbelievable scrutiny
and we are never free
We stay because we forget how the moon illuminates
We stay because we can no longer hear the river's song
We stay because we have been fighting for far too long
and we are tired.

When He Died

Robin Rogers

I got a call from camp that every mother dreads. My son is unhappy and wants to come home. There is a boy, he told me, who is mentally challenged. Then, sobbing, he burst out, "And he reminds me of Dad." I'd later call the camp and learn that this boy—who was by all accounts, including my son's, very sweet—did odd things. The other campers would sing the camp song. This boy would sing his own song.

"No one understands but you," my son said to me softly.

"Look, the building is crying," my ex-husband said to me, looking out the window at the rain against the neighboring building. I stopped and looked at him. Was this a beautiful thing to say, or was it strange? In our basement, he collected doors that he found on the street, more than sixty of them. He had buckets of doorknobs and so much furniture that it spilled into the backyard, the backyard where he kept food hidden, in case he was hungry.

In the walls of our old building, he stored more furniture. Broken fish tanks, old crutches. I never knew where much of it came from. One day, I looked out the window and saw him pushing a bright-orange shopping cart down the street. He had on safety goggles and was grinning wildly. *He should stop that,* I thought. *The neighbors will think he is crazy.*

He carved topiaries into his beard. A kaleidoscopic web of wires and strings crossed the ceiling of his basement workshop, where he spent all of his time. "Each string," he would later tell me, tapping his temple with his index finger, "is attached to my brain." He had always had a spotty work history, but his highly paid jobs lasted for years at first. Then they lasted for months, for weeks, and then, finally, for hours.

"I am more enlightened than Buddha," he told me earnestly one day. "Closer to God than Jesus," he explained a different day.

"When did he die?" a holistic healer asked. I could remember almost to the day when he sat catatonic on our old, green sofa. He sat for days. Pregnant with the boy now calling me from camp, I thought, *It is depression.* "How did you know?" I asked the healer, as my tears poured forward. She gave me a soft smile, "My mother was schizophrenic."

When people die, there are rituals. People comfort the family. They eat cake together. No one brings a cake when your mentally ill husband breaks from reality. My family of four became a family of three: two boys and me. We bought a dog. A neighbor who had seen my ex-husband forcibly removed from the house by the police commented, in a thick Polish accent, "Dogs are good for boys."

People said I was divorced. I felt widowed.

My ex-husband wanders around a small town three hours from our home. Nothing is the same, but everything is the same. I still get the phone calls that break every mother's heart: "I'm homesick, Mom." But there is a twist: "He reminds me of Dad." Their father is a ghost presence in my boys' lives. Mine, too. I sometimes wish someone would reach out to us and say, "I'm sorry for your loss."

I try to decide if I will pick up my son from camp early. "It is important to show him that he can handle this on his own," the child psychiatrist says, with more certainty than I think is warranted. "Don't leave him there," my mother pleads with me over the phone. "He needs you." I drive three hours to the camp, park my little car in a gravelly parking lot, and walk over to an unmanicured field full of roughhousing children. There is my boy. Frozen. His coppery hair glinting in the sun. He sees me, rushes toward me, and throws his skinny arms and legs around me sobbing so hard that he cannot speak. There is no boyish bravado. No pre-teen self-consciousness.

"Should we get some pizza?" I ask. He nods, yes. "And then we will come back for your bags?" I say. He nods, yes, again, and we amble off to the car.

Over pizza that afternoon, my son and I talked about his father. My son didn't have a father to push him to be good in sports, he told me, and all of the other boys were better at them than him. We talked about his loss in his words.

I don't know if I made the right decision when I took him home that day or if I said the right things as we lingered over undercooked pizza in that small Massachusetts town. What I do know is that I talked about my ex-husband's condition openly and honestly, and I will continue to talk about it openly and honestly. It is true that there are no sympathy cards for when you lose a husband to mental illness. No one sends condolences. But still, I think my son can't be right when he says, "No one understands but you." There must be more of us, but we are very, very quiet, like we are walking in a cemetery.

Being the wife, mother, daughter, or sister of someone who is incarcerated is like membership in a secret society—a secret society of women warriors who journey hundreds of miles under the cover of night, who bare their souls in monitored phone calls and scrutinized letters, who bring rays of love to dismal brick-and-mortar visitors floors, and who shine as beacons of hope in the most hopeless of circumstances.

—Terri Linton

This Lesson I Know
My Boy Already Knows

Georgia Pearle

Somewhere West a combine
   is crushing new mice,
And my freshman son needs
   help with Steinbeck,

And tomorrow we'll catch
   the 84 bus to the redline
to the 40 bus before sunrise,
   and my daughter will nod

in the crook of my armpit,
   her young breath still
full of spearmint: she won't notice
   the shadows that shuffle

beneath each overpass we pass.
    I don't think about that
Christmas when I signed
    the charity papers *homeless*

when we wait at the next bus stop
    where there are three ageless,
white and gaunt, picking through
    butts on the sidewalk

they murmur together, *my corner*
    that bitch got my corner
and I mouth to my boy, *meth,*
    which he knows only

as the smoke that took his father
    to some unknowable world
but he knows the look I strike
    means huddle closer, trust

nothing near us, save our own
    spared feet and step quickly
do not ask me where we're going
    boy step quickly toward dawn

But tonight he is writing on Lenny
    and George, and tonight I bide
my tongue. I say nothing of men
    not knowing their strength.

from *The Light of the World: A Memoir*

Elizabeth Alexander

I have not yet learned how to use our television DVR. One of the points of marriage is that you split labor. In the olden days that meant one hunted and one gathered; now it means one knows where the tea-towels are kept and the other knows how to program the DVR, for why should we both have to know?

I now learn the DVR and find traces of him in the programming. Under Record Series, Melissa Harris-Perry's new show. Oh how he loved a smart black girl, and especially a cute one. Kundalini Yoga. *Nova. American Masters. Unsung*, just for me. I'd binge-watch his offerings (Lou Rawls! Donna Summer! Shalamar!). My Negro wife, he'd say, with the warmest of amused smiles.

Now I erase some of those settings to make room for new things: NBA All-Star Game, *Scandal, Chopped*. I erase *The Big C*; that show is over, and on it, the middle-aged wife died. The husband had a heart attack and lived. I watched the end of that show that Ficre and I started together without him, and wept, cursing the living husband who came back from the precipice.

He was never not thinking about us. Everything he touched contained his thoughts of us, including the alien television.

I speak on the phone for the last time I will need to to a cardiologist who explains to me what happened exactly as others have, based on his autopsy report: he was probably dead before he hit the ground, that he may have felt a bit sick beforehand but the event itself was like lightning, and would not have left time for fear or pain.

Then he tells me the story of the priest who had a heart attack on the pulpit while preaching the resurrection on Easter, and the church was next to the fire department, and they came instantly and helped him, and he lived, and then later told of going to the precipice. He saw his mother. It was peaceful and beautiful. He was sorry to come back.

I keep paying his cell phone bill for a year and a half afterwards, because I don't want to lose the text messages, but I don't have the heart to read and transfer them. The phone goes dead and gets lost somewhere in the house.

But then I find it, and it is time. Simon cries rainstorm tears when he sees the photograph on the phone of his father blowing out his birthday candles at the kitchen table.

Texts he sent at 2:08 p.m. the day he died, to one of our nieces, Luuwam, about her mother's medical treatment.

A short bit later, texts with Solo, saying that he was waiting for the boys in the parking lot at school.

What a profound mystery it is to me, the vibrancy of presence, the realness of it, and then, gone. Ficre not at the kitchen table seems impossible. I draft my first meager poem in many months, a re-entry exercise:

FAMILY IN 3/4 TIME

We are now a three-legged table,
a family of three, once a family of four.
We bring ourselves into new balance.
The table wobbles, but does not fall.

We are still a family of four, I think,
when we meet new people, and wonder
if Ficre is visible to them.
I keep the kitchen table set for four

and buy the same amount of food: four
salmon filets, eight thin chicken cutlets,
four miniature chocolate eclairs.
We are ready for when he returns.

I watch a short video the children took on Ficre's iPhone from the morning of his fiftieth birthday. He is asleep and I am circled around him, pretending to sleep, for I am in on the surprise. The boys bring a tray to our bed: a daffodil (from the garden; it is March 21), espresso pot, toast, white yogurt drizzled with golden honey, and strawberries. All of us in our bed eat together, everything important and true in that image. Solo is the cameraman. Simon tells joke after joke, and the boys fall out laughing. One of them sings a song.

Hope is not about proving anything. It's about choosing to believe this one thing—that love is bigger than any grim bleak shit anyone can throw at us.

—Anne Lamott

Then

Ruth Stone

That summer, from the back porch,
we would hear the storm like a train,
the Doppler effect compressing the air;
the rain, a heavy machine, coming up
from below the orchard, rushing toward us.
My trouble was I could not keep you dead.
You entered even the inanimate,
returning in endless guises.
And that winter an ermine moved into the house.
It was so cold the beams cracked.
The ermine's fur was creamy white
with the last half of the tail soot black.
Its body about ten inches long,
it slipped through small holes.
It watched us from a high shelf in the kitchen.
In our loss we accepted the strange shape of things

as though it had a meaning for us,
as though we moved slowly over the acreage,
as though the ground modulated like water.
The floors and the cupboards slanted to the West,
the house sinking toward the evening side of the sky.
The children and I sitting together waiting,
there on the back porch, the massive engine
of the storm swelling up through the undergrowth,
pounding toward us.

When Black Lives Matter More Than You Ever Imagined

Deborah Oster Pannell

A young black man living in the South Bronx, on his way home from school one day, my future husband was stopped in the front vestibule of his apartment building by a police officer who put a gun to his head, insisted he place his hands against the wall, then searched his backpack that was filled with nothing but schoolbooks and homework.

I grew up a train ride and a world away from all that, a white, middle-class dentist's daughter, the beneficiary of the master plan that was the racially segregated suburbs of Long Island.

Despite our vastly different backgrounds, once my husband and I turned our sights on each other, I was helpless in his orbit and pledged myself to him, digging into our relationship with a fierce loyalty that lasted twenty-two years. We created our own unique way of living in the world.

Yet our union was forged out of struggle almost from the beginning. Living with sickle cell disease, a chronic, genetic condition, my husband had to forge a warrior-like character. We joked that his autobiography should be called *Black, Sick, and Poor.*

Sickle cell anemia requires a strong narcotic medication to deal with its chief symptom, acute pain episodes. If you know anything about racial bias in medical treatment, you can imagine what a shit show that is. Once a doctor refused to give him medication in the midst of a severe pain crisis, accusing him of faking his symptoms. The doctor actually said the words "because you're a drug addict." Another time, a medical team wanted to withhold pain medication until they administered a spinal tap, sticking a long needle in his spine to draw out fluid, to determine the cause of his fever (or, more likely, to give an intern a chance to practice the procedure).

We discovered early on that my status as a white lady helped fight the inevitable stereotypes and ensured that doctors filled his prescriptions. I ran interference in all kinds of situations, working the hospital hierarchy to get my husband the proper and humane treatment he required and deserved.

In some ways, at twenty-something years old, I was ignorant of what I was walking into, both in my choice of life partner and in our eventual decision to have a child. But my trip through the medical system with my husband brought a quick dose of reality, and in the following years, navigating the public school system with our son would sober me up even more.

I've seen my black son characterized as a misbehaving kid in nursery school, while his similarly acting blond-haired, blue-eyed best friend was treated like a delightful free spirit. I've seen my son treated with suspicion and hostility by teachers and other authority figures, even when his behavior did nothing to warrant such treatment. I've seen him feel the discouragement of being cast in the role of thug before his accusers even had the chance to know him. I've also watched him struggle with the urge to act the part, to fulfill the worst expectations of those who expect nothing better from him.

Over the years, as my experiences as wife and mother deepened my understanding of white privilege, I've learned both the influence and the limits of my white lady powers. They helped make certain aspects of my husband's life easier, but in the end, they couldn't save him from the ravages of his disease—he died in 2009, at the age of forty-five. Although I have been able to step in and advocate for my son, finding him the best possible educational environment—a small, intentional, and creative community dedicated to his well-being and all-around development, appreciative of his unique needs and unconventional rhythms—I cannot guarantee his safety in the world.

Remember Tamir Rice, the twelve-year-old boy holding a toy gun in a playground, who was gunned down by a Cleveland rookie police officer in 2014? His name brings shudders of dread to anyone raising a black child. In the face of this fear, what can I do? Only recently did I learn that it's basically a given that parents of black children have to teach their kids how to survive a police encounter. My white privilege had allowed my ignorance in that regard.

For me, "Black Lives Matter" is not merely a slogan or a political position. It is the embodiment of the love I feel for my family and friends. It is my blood, my breath, my normal, my dream. I persist in my belief in the power of love. My desire to disentangle myself and my son from the reactionary, generational web of trauma, the grip of epigenetic memory, drives me forward with optimism despite the awfulness that seems to be growing all around us.

Yes, I am frightened—terrified, in fact—by the hatred and fury I see spreading around the world. But I'm a mother. My job, as I see it, is to raise my son into the kind of man who will disrupt this destructive cycle and make a positive contribution to the world.

When my husband died, my son was six years old. To him the loss of his dad came as if in a dream. "Are you sure?" he asked, when

I told him his daddy had died. How does a boy make sense of the sudden loss of his father's constant companionship, a presence he has felt since before birth? How does he comprehend the absence of a man who made it his life's mission to be remembered as his son's dad, not his sick dad—the one who tutored him for three hours after school (in kindergarten), the one who had lightsaber duels with him in the front yard and snuck him candies when his mom wasn't looking? How does this white mom guide her black son toward adulthood?

At the age of sixteen, my son has lived more years without his father than with him. He is on the cusp of manhood at a time when the world may demand of him—of us all—sacrifices of the highest order. So we move forward, he and I, embodying what we believe is right, inspired by the powerful spirit of the man who left us.

In a Quiet Moment

Hilary Melton

In a quiet moment,
maybe a sunny day drive
alone,

it can slip in before I notice—
imagining myself if
he were dead.

And sometimes, unable to stop
screaming,
my vocal cords snap.

Other times—I sleep
through the night, pack a bag
and hitchhike to Montreal.

Still
if I could go now—as if he
never happened—
to a store selling ten-year-olds

and browse through the selection:
smart ones, athletic ones,
well-behaved ones

and one in the corner—

there humming tunelessly
glancing this way and that
following light and shadows

those Elizabeth Taylor blue eyes
that one-sided smile—

I'd point and say,
him.

Heroin, Rain

Anne Spollen

I am driving on the Garden State Parkway at eleven o'clock at night, in dense rain that sweeps sideways. My daughter sleeps in the back seat. My son sits next to me, nodding in and out. I count miles between hospital signs.

I have never before driven through darkness in blinding rain.

My hands shake. I try to control their tremor. If I can control my hands, I can control my thoughts. If I can control my thoughts, I can control the car. If I can control the car, I can control not having an accident. I keep thinking of that book, *If You Give a Moose a Muffin* . . .

A sign flashes overhead: *Warning Limited Visibility*.

Perfect.

My son looks over at me. "What did you do today?" For a second, he is alert, breathing regularly. Then he drifts off again.

I don't want to tell him that all day, a thread of fear about him spidered across my thoughts and I knew, in my soul, that he was not all right.

"Hard to drive in the rain, isn't it?" He looks out the window after asking, already disconnected from his words.

"It is."

I don't tell him that his cat has escaped the hastily made cardboard transport box and has wedged himself in the space between my neck and the headrest. Ozzy's claws open onto my shoulder. I can't move for fear that he will razor them into my flesh.

A tractor-trailer honks at me, jarring my son awake. He opens his eyes, startled, then shuts them.

"What does it look like to you?" I ask. "The headlights. The rain makes them all dreamy looking."

"It's pretty cool." He grins, then his head is down again. I listen to make sure he is breathing.

That's the way it is with heroin.

I have always been mystically connected to my middle child, sensing when things were not right with him. During his childhood, I would feel dread, and moments later, the school nurse or principal would call. As he got older, he joked how I called at the exact moment he was getting pulled over or into some other kind of trouble. When he disappeared to drink or use, I combed the woods with radar-like instincts, always finding him. Now, at eighteen, he rarely called, but all that day, I had been having those familiar feelings of dread. When the phone rang that night, I was not surprised.

"Sup, Mom?" He sounded like he was speaking through one of those distortion programs they use in crime shows to mask voices. He exhaled. Music. Laughter. "You should come over."

He said this despite the fact that I was at least ninety minutes and a state away.

The terms of his probation require him to stay in New Jersey, at his dad's house. It's an active user's dream there: a frat house atmosphere with no rules and a laxity toward legality.

"I want you to come back to my house. You can't stay at dad's tonight."

Fear runs beneath his few words. Tonight, something is very wrong.

With addiction, the unspoken speaks the loudest.

When my daughter and I arrive almost two hours later, my son stands in the foyer, moving like he's underwater.

"Wow, that was like only a few minutes."

He points to a towel-lined box where his cat sleeps. "I didn't want Ozzy to get cold."

I hug him.

"What are we doing?" my daughter asks. At fourteen, she is viscerally aware of her brother's use. Her gaze is expectant.

"Leaving." I say this one word with certainty.

I am glad she doesn't ask me what we are doing after that.

On the drive back, inside a dark howl of rain, with Ozzy's claws playing staccato on my neck and one eye on my son's level of alertness, I know I have to do something drastic. I've taken him to the hospital at least four times when he was high only to have his father retrieve him and begin the cycle over again. This time, we need to try in-patient.

Elated by the promise of this new solution, I choose to ignore that I have no idea how to arrange in-patient care. I drive a little faster until I see that the Outerbridge, the only bridge I know to get home, is closed. I follow signs, but end up on a desolate road in an industrial area. Around us, cranes and metallic machinery loom like the setting of a post-apocalyptic movie.

"We're lost." My son points to the GPS that reads *Acquiring Signal.*

"Just a detour." I say this as we turn down another dead end street. For a few seconds, I pull over and rest my head on the steering wheel. I listen to the sound of my children breathing, feel the slight sharpness of cat claws grazing my neck. I close my eyes. In the bottom of my stomach, a weight gathers, small and dense, the mass of a black hole.

What I would give for a goddamned map.

"Mom?" my daughter's voice calls, full of sleep.

"Detour," I say, starting the car. "We're good."

I glide the car in reverse and head toward a blurry streak of lights. And there it is: a sign for another bridge entrance.

I believe I am the only woman who ever cried when she saw the Goethals Bridge.

While the kids sleep, I call every rehab center I can.

Nothing.

Finally, a call is returned at 5:30 am. Could I get him to Florida?

I tell the man, "I have $180 to my name."

"He's going to be dope-sick when he wakes up," the man says. Then, miraculously, "I can send a paid ticket to your email."

"When?"

"Now."

I tell my son, who at first refuses. I take his face in my hands. "You have to go," I say in the voice I used when he was a child and he had to take medicine or share a favorite toy. Only now I cannot make him do anything; he is legally an adult.

I hold my breath.

In the second miracle of that night, he agrees.

That afternoon, I watch my son's plane rise until I can no longer see it. I want to stop here, say that he went to treatment and now he's well. Only that's not the way it is with heroin: there would be more crazed nights, more arrests, more driving through rain, more rehabs, more enabling from his dad, more long periods where I could not reach him.

But as I stood watching that plane disappear, at least for those moments, I knew I had driven through wind and rain and darkness without navigation, with closed bridges and piercing cat claws, unsure of how to take care of him or my daughter or myself, and I was, for the first time that I could remember, alone. Truly alone.

And we had come out of it for the better. I felt stronger, less afraid.

No one was ever going to give me a map or guarantee passage over any bridge or pledge that my child would survive this disease. But at least I could pilot through heroin and rain and frantic all-night phone calls to find wings that would lift him from darkness, if only temporarily. And for now, that would have to keep us.

On Home

Lisa Fay Coutley

All winter long my sons have pointed guns
in my face and with their mouths popped

the triggers. The oldest wants to spoon me.
The youngest wants to change his name

to *the playground pimp*. When we circle up
for dinner, I'm careful not to say chicken *breast*

or meat*ball* or anything they can follow with
that's what she said. Consider the going rate

for hormones, then picture an eager group
of eBay bidders. I joke, but someone should

tell these boys—in a wake of black mascara,
mothers drive away. All winter long I've left

feel-good Post-its on the bathroom mirror,
the espresso maker, the edge of my razor.

Every day, I've given myself reasons to stay.

What I Will Tell His Daughter, When She's Old Enough to Ask

Meg Day

When they removed the yellow tape
from the doorway, our neckless birds
still sat, unfolding, on the tabletop,

his stack of paper—foils & florals
& one tartan velum—fanning out
across *Origami for Dummies*

& onto the floor. The chair we'd set
in the middle of the room for hanging
the first twenty attempts at a thousand

seemed frozen mid-bow, all four legs facing
west. He never mentioned his plans
or his grief—only that I could find the fishing

line toward the front, near the large spools
of rope. *Don't go on without me*, I'd said
& whistled the eleven short blocks

back from the hardware while he folded his apologies
& suspended himself from the ceiling of cranes.

Grey Street

Angela Ricketts

NOVEMBER 21, 2010

Sometimes when you wake in the middle of the night it's only for a slippery moment, a moment to re-cozy yourself, to remember with a flash of panic that forgotten appointment from the day before or to get up to potty. "Potty" is a word mothers begin using from the instant they give birth and that never leaves their vocabulary until death. Sometimes what wakes you is a long-forgotten memory, the thing you tried to put behind you.

Once or twice in a lifetime you wake up and just know it: You are dying, even though three hours ago you were watching *Weeds* and fluffing pillows on the couch and wiping down the kitchen counter-tops because you never know what the night will bring. And because a perfectly neat home masks the other mess that spins beyond control.

I jerk awake and move the empty wine glass to see the time on the digital clock. Two something. I should remember the precise time on the clock, but I am a date person. Dates I remember; times, not so much.

In the silent house with a staring cat and three sleeping children and again without a husband present, I struggle through sleepy, disoriented eyes to remember where I am. A sweet artificial stank hangs in the air; oh yeah, the Yankee Candle I blew out before I slammed the last gulp of wine. Nothing looks familiar as I go back and forth in my mind; which issue is more pressing, the crushing pain in my chest or where the hell I am? The glare of the streetlight shining into the window reminds me I'm home, home for now. This is our third house in less than two years, and it takes me a minute to remember where I am. Fort Campbell. Just across the Tennessee border, but with a Kentucky address, surely the result of a political fight over which state got to claim ownership of the home of the 101st Airborne. I'm back in the familiar zone I like to think of as Grey Street, a favorite Dave Matthews song about a woman who feels numbed and paralyzed by her life. Like her world has spiraled beyond her control. Where colors bleed and overlap into only gray. The vibrancy of each color not lost, just absorbed into a blanket of grayness. The gray of autopilot. The gray of another deployment, of a home with a man of the house who wouldn't know which drawer held the spoons. He's the man of the house in concept alone. He is three months into a yearlong deployment in Afghanistan, with no need to even own a house key.

But in this two-something wee hour, these ideas are just whispers under my blankets and inside my skin. My feet nudge around looking for the children, who sometimes wander half asleep into my bed. As soon as I move I feel it, the thing that startled me awake. It isn't a dream or a memory or a forgotten appointment. It's pain, the physical kind. What frightens me in that moment isn't the gripping pain in my chest, but a wave of incomprehensible terror for its newness and unfamiliar nature. A twisting stab in my back pushes me out of bed and to my feet. I feel sweat roll down the back of my neck, but it's almost Thanksgiving and I allow the chill from outside to come into our home at night. I prefer the insulation of blankets and flannel pajamas to warm air.

Oh, hell. It's a panic attack. My body is at long last going on strike, revolting from the stress of eight long, intense deployments. That's what I've been warned of, anyway, in the "resiliency" workshops and briefings army wives sit through during deployments. Well, before deployments, during deployments, and after deployments. So all the time. Whatever you face or feel, surely it's addressed in a binder somewhere. The army's philosophy is that just by virtue of identifying and labeling an issue, it's 95 percent fixed. At each available opportunity, we are reminded to pace ourselves and manage stress. I picture the PowerPoint slide: "Panic attacks are a terrifying but normal reaction: It will feel like you are going to die, but here are coping tips. . . . Remember, we are ARMY STRONG!" But what were the tips? Dammit. Breathe. That's surely one. I do feel like I'm going to die.

I grab my cell phone off the dresser and wander through the upstairs of our quiet house. Joe is almost a teenager, a stack of *Call of Duty: Black Ops* video games just inches from his sleeping head and a game controller teetering on the edge of the bed. The violent video games that Jack allowed because they are a reality of his job. Jack argued that the video games are disturbing with their accuracy and not gratuitous in their violence. The line between good guys and bad guys is clear, at least in the game.

Our two daughters, Bridget, who is ten, and Greta, five, are curled together in Bridget's room across the hall. Using the term "our" is an effort on my part. "My children" comes more naturally; I have to make an effort to remind myself that these are "our children." I'm not alone in parenting, at least not in theory. In reality, yes, I am alone.

In this moment of defining chest pain I am alone.

The blinding streetlight streams into the adjacent rooms and onto my sleeping babies. Sometimes, when morning comes, I find all three kids together in one bed, or all of us in my bed. But this is how they landed tonight.

My left shoulder pangs and I grip the wall without a sound. Just my palm on the ugly wall. For years the army painted the inside of our homes chalky white; then they decided to get all snazzy with the neutral tones.

At the bottom of the stairs, our wedding portrait hangs, and the light hits my neck in the photo just perfectly. I bought that double strand of mock pearls intending to wear them choker style with the wedding dress that I thought was so simple compared with the other dresses in the early 1990s. When my wedding day finally arrived, I was thankful beyond measure that the pearls were adjustable and could hang loosely around my neck instead of high on my throat. The latter would have been prettier, more chic. But I couldn't bear it. Couldn't bear to have anything choke me.

There's some warning signal about shoulder pain I should remember now. I flounder down the stairs. Calling 911 never enters my mind. Drama queens, attention whores, that's who calls 911 in the middle of the night in our neighborhood. According to post policy, Joe is officially old enough to babysit. It occurs to me to just drive to the hospital myself and no one would even know I was gone.

"Did you hear all that commotion last night was Angie Hawkins? She called 911 for a freaking panic attack at two a.m. Two fire trucks, an ambulance, and three MP cars. Woke up the whole block for a panic attack. And on a school night. She's just trying to get her husband sent home." Some roll their eyes and some shake their heads. The scenario of tomorrow's bus stop conversation fuels my confidence that I can drive the two miles to the hospital on my own and get back before the kids even wake for school. No one will know. I can save the story of my middle-of-the-night panic attack for a boring moment during Bunco or a punch line at the next coffee.

With too many symptoms to focus on them separately any-more, I grow weak and fight tears as the pain radiates back and forth from my spine to my left shoulder. One ugly green Croc lying by the door will have to do as I head to the car with one bare foot. Maybe I shouldn't leave the kids. What if they wander into my bed and I'm not there? The thought crosses my mind but dissipates in my brief hunt for the matching Croc. The hospital on post is two miles away, a straight shot without a single car on the road. I drive right past the emergency entrance and drive over the grass to turn around. Not even an MP on the empty roads that are usually peppered with at least one officer on each block, waiting to catch me blow through stop signs or drive on the grass. Just my luck. Not an MP in sight.

I don't bother to park, leaving my car running and the driver's door hanging open. I stumble into automatic ER doors and explode into tears. "I'm dying." I half expect a reprimand and an order to move my car before I die. My mask of strength is torn from my face.

"What's your name? Where is your ID card? Are you allergic to anything? Are you going to vomit? Where is the pain coming from? Rate your pain from one to ten. Ma'am, can you breathe?" But this ER tech says these words in a far-too-unaffected way. The workers behind the desk share glances, and a moment of embarrassment rushes over me and then past me. I want to scream at them that I was not stung by an imaginary bee and am not suffering from an imagined allergic reaction. They will realize it soon enough, and I will enjoy a moment of satisfaction, if I live that long. Somehow that's all preferable to a panic attack.

A heart attack leaves me in the ICU for a week. Not a cardiac event, but a full-fledged heart attack that leaves my heart compromised forever and leads to surreal discussions about a long-term prognosis. Cardiologists scratched their heads over what could have caused such an absurdity. Weeks earlier, I had jogged six miles up and down a mountain. I never touched a cigarette. I squeezed my size 8 ass into size 6 jeans. A heart attack?

Hours later in the cardiac catheterization lab, my last memory is the anesthesiologist reviewing my chart, reciting my age, weight, family history, general health information. He looks at me and shakes his head. A nurse in the frenzy of prepping the operating room flips on a CD player, AC/DC's "Hells Bells." I'd like to laugh at her ironic song choice. Even through my morphine stupor, I marvel, watching the fluidity of the staff's second-nature routine as a team. Not unlike army wives. Just before I drift into the bliss of anesthesia, my final memory is of the white-haired, jolly-looking anesthesiologist leaning close to my ear and asking me, "Why are you on this table? What broke your heart?"

Chapter Five:
A Change Is Gonna Come

And the time came when the risk to remain tight in a bud was more painful than the risk it took to blossom.

—Anaïs Nin

Now That I Am Forever with Child

Audre Lorde

How the days went
while you were blooming within me
I remember   each upon each
the swelling changed planes of my body

how you first fluttered   then jumped
and I thought it was my heart.

How the days wound down
and the turning of winter
I recall   you
growing heavy against the wind.
I thought   now her hands

are formed   her hair
has started to curl
now her teeth are done
now she sneezes.

Then the seed opened.
I bore you one morning
just before spring
my head rang like a fiery piston
my legs were towers between which
a new world was passing.

Since then
I can only distinguish
one thread within running hours
you   flowing through selves
toward You.

Coming Out Pregnant!

Staceyann Chin

Everyone in my building knows I'm a dyke: largely because I have lived in the same Brooklyn building for more than a decade. In that time I have been the odd girl with the wild hair, the barefoot woman comparing mangoes and the flesh of a woman on Broadway, the quirky lesbian who changes girlfriends every two years or so, and finally, I thought, established homosexual neighbor, part of eclectic landscape, known, tolerated, even accepted. Over time, I have become a fixture in this big old community that is quickly suffering the ravages of gentrification. Old women from the Caribbean are used to my flirting with them on the elevator; telling them they are not allowed to look this fly on such a nice summer day, "Don't you know lesbians live in the building, Mrs. Johnson?" They usually blush, and beam, and tell me I should behave: "Don't you see I'm too old for anybody (man or woman) to look at me dat way, child."

The Black boys who grew up on the block are respectful. Their eyes may light up and ogle the gorgeous women who come in and out of the multicolored apartment on the 4th floor, but they are always careful of what they say out loud. They tell me how much they like the view, but assure me they don't have sticky fingers. The old men are reserved, but polite. The plethora of younger, middle-class, Asian, queer-identified hipster folks, who pay way too much for these under-serviced apartments, wave and smile and tell me how pleased they are to be living in a building that already has an LGBT person. The new White residents, complete with alabaster skin, blond hair, and designer dogs, confess quietly in the foyer that they've read my book, or seen one of my shows. Friends in the building tell me of the gossip they've heard about the kooky Jamaican girl in the lime green cargo pants who only dates women. In a pleasant sort of way, I thought myself done with coming out, especially inside my own communities.

Then I got a baby bump, and promptly perplexed my collection of very diverse friends, neighbors, and acquaintances.

The moment I began to show, people started doing undercover double takes, especially in the elevator. The building is old, so the ride up is very, very slow. People sort of talk normally to me, but they no longer look in my face, or at my boobs. They stare straight ahead and glance sideways at my protruding stomach every ten seconds or so. Not one person has taken the plunge and asked outright if I was pregnant. Not even when I have been sick, and spitting up in Ziploc bags, did anyone query why I was hurling into a plastic bag two minutes before I got into my apartment. People just talked about the weather, or the economy, or the fact that the new White people are complaining that the heat in the building is too high and now management has turned down the heat and the rest of us Black folk are freezing.

Finally I got tired of the weird glances and started explaining, unasked, that I was four months pregnant, or five months along, or expecting a baby in January, and that I am on bed rest and that I have been vomiting for the entire seven months I have been knocked up.

People try to hide how surprised they are. I can see them swallow the questions and blink back how confused they feel. I almost enjoy seeing them journey from "Aren't you a lesbian?" to "Are you going with men now?" to "Aww, shizzle, I can't ask her any of those questions so I might as well smile and nod."

One woman I told shrieked, in an eerily squeaky voice, "Lord Jesus! I dunno why this elevator smelling so stuffy these days. I think I go make a complaint to management about it today." Then she told me she liked my shoes and hastily exited the lift.

The silence is immediate when I happen upon a group of tenants gathered in the lobby. Everyone nods and waves and watches as I slowly waddle my way to the car parked on the street out front.

Most of the other LGBT faces offer up congratulations, until they find out I'm doing it without a partner or co-parent. Lips are pursed. Sighs are delivered. And then silence ensues. They don't approve. Some of the braver ones go on to say, "Well, I would never choose to do it that way—not that I think anything is wrong with it. It just doesn't seem right to me. But I suppose if you believe you can do it . . . " That long pause is usually followed with questions about why I didn't adopt. Apparently, single parenthood is okay for kids without anyone, but somehow unacceptable as a biological choice.

Some people are less tongue-tied than my immediate neighbors. They just blurt out whatever comes to mind. "Shoot, Staceyann! I thought you was a lesbian! How dat happened?"

Straight men (especially if they are religious or of color) tend to be very offended, or very proud. "I don't see why you need to have children by a man if you don't want us that way. I believe you give up the right to have children if you don't want to go with a man. You tricked some poor man into thinking you straight, didn't you?" Or, "I knew it! I knew you would cross back over! You too sexy to be a lesbian! I mean, look at your breasts! And your shape! I knew you would find a man to turn you normal!"

Sometimes I walk away. But I really want to punch them and stomp on them and tell them how bigoted they are. More often than not, I say in a calm voice that I paid to have myself artificially inseminated at a fertility clinic. When I am feeling confrontational, I tell them I bought the sperm from a homeless man who needed money for his girlfriend's third abortion. This usually sends them into cardiac arrest, which renders them silent just long enough for me to escape. Or it makes them pop a religious vein and spew a series of even more ignorant responses, about the unnaturalness of artificial methods of reproduction, how God did not intend that children be made in test tubes.

Straight women look at me with a combination of pity and anger. Many of them haven't found Mr. Right yet, and the biological clock is also tick-tick-ticking away for them. They want children, but so many are unable to shake how they were raised to make the choice to have a child on their own. To them it's a failure to concede the hunt for a good husband. They usually make comments like, "I'm not sure children were meant to be raised without both parents. I mean, if something happens, like, say, a parent dies or the father leaves and decides not to be there for the child, well, that's different. That's playing the hand you were dealt. But to intentionally rob a child of a father . . . I just don't know that that is a good thing."

I even had one woman tell me that the IVF is why I am having all these problems with my pregnancy. That God must not be pleased with the artificial seed growing inside me. She went as far as to suggest the child could have birth defects and learning problems and gender confusion because I did not lay with a man as God has decreed for women to do.

It took me about ten seconds to restrain myself, to decide not to slap this person in the face for wishing ill on the child I already adore more than I have ever adored anyone. I quickly remind myself that a physical altercation with this nitwit would only further stress my already taxed body. I wish I could explain to every idiot who says some stupid crap like that how proud I am of my choice to become pregnant. I wish I could show them how it has changed me, made me more of everything, more of myself. I am thinking of getting cards printed with a prepared rant of some kind, complete with choice cuss words, to hand out when folks get ahead of themselves.

It's a veritable minefield just walking outside.

I am on bed rest and don't get out that often, so it's always a shock to me to have folks respond so strongly to my pregnancy. And now that my belly is miles ahead of the rest of me, everybody knows on sight about my condition, which means I have no control over people's reactions. Old women smile and ask how far along I am. Touchy-feely granola types touch my belly uninvited and offer to give me reiki to open some chakra or other. Strangers assume me heterosexual and ask me about my husband, or "the father." They are quite confused when I say I used a donor, that this kid does not have a father. Even in my obstetrician's office I have to constantly correct the nurses who insist on calling me Mrs. Chin. One day I got so tired of it that I sat up in my chair and shouted from the back of the room, "Nurse, I have told you a hundred times. I am not married. I am a single lesbian who got pregnant by artificial insemination. I don't have a husband. I don't have a boyfriend. I don't even have a girlfriend. I'm doing this solo, so I'm definitely not a Mrs. anything. So could you please remember to say Ms. Chin?"

She mumbled an apology and handed me my receipt. As I walked back to my chair I reveled in the discomfort of the "legitimately pregnant" heterosexual women squirming in their chairs and avoiding my eyes. Later that day I got an email from a woman thanking me for speaking out. She is forty-four years old, a lesbian, and she did an IVF pregnancy. She said she could never be that out about her process, but that it made her feel visible to hear me articulate it in that space with such pride. Her note brought home the irony of me assuming everyone in that waiting room heterosexual while I was protesting others doing the same to me.

But the coming out process continues. In ways I never imagined. Mid-examination, medical personnel will ask if daddy and I have been abstaining, as is recommended for women who are placenta previa. The forms in the hospitals all require father's name and mother's name, never just a partner. They suggest you ask him to do this or include him in that, or talk to him about something or the other. Friends and family members speak of my donor as the baby's father, or the baby-daddy. There is no room for the woman who has decided to do this alone. The registries in the three places I am registered, buybuybaby.com, target.com, and babiesrus.com, all have advice for what to do with your partner as you prepare for "the shared joy of your baby's birth."

I find myself saying, over and over again, "No. I'm lesbian, so I don't have a male partner. And yes, I'm single, so I will be doing this alone. And I must point out that 'alone' does not mean I don't have help. I expect my vast village of friends to be a part of our lives. But there is no father, no partner, no husband, no lover. Legal responsibilities are solely mine." Every day, I find myself needing to affirm that this was a willing choice, that though I may have moments of doubt or loneliness, I'm largely at peace with my path. I have to assure all sorts of people that this baby is wanted, is loved, and will be amply provided for with respect to diapers, discipline, and encouragement, and the space to be whatever he or she can be in our not-so-traditional family.

Because difficult or not, shared joy or sweet sorrow in solitude, I am awaiting his arrival, preparing for her presence, knowing with everything in me how proud I am, how lucky I am, to be a single, Black, self-employed, radical, progressive, lesbian artist who is thirty-one weeks pregnant with a child she has wanted for more than a decade. That miracle is in itself a thing to celebrate, even if the experience has sent me back, reeling, to traverse the coming out process yet another time.

The Story, for Now

Janlori Goldman

No father. That's what I told you.
    By second grade, friends said
        all kids have one, somewhere,

called you *liar.* The difference between *biology*
    and *Dad*? That's the story that grew
        as you grew, like dated pencil marks

on the doorframe. Now I tell you—
    I met him on a work trip.
        In the morning, we circled Henry Moore's

massive, marble women.
    In other cities we'd meet for Greek food,
        fool around. *A divorce.*

He said he was getting one. I said,
    you should know. I'm going to have this baby.
      I'm not asking you for anything.

I knew nothing of asking.
    All I knew, the gift was in me,
      even if he didn't mean to give it.

He looked at the mound under my sweater—
    you can always make another. This one
      will ruin my life. The wife and I,

we're trying to work things out.
    He needed me to keep a secret,
      and I could only see my way

to one very sure place of going it alone.
    I agreed to *No Father*,
      just xxxxxxxxx on your birth certificate.

When you're very young I give you this story:
    a friend helped me. A woman
      needs sperm to make a baby—

this is true the way a story with a missing piece
    can be true. By twelve, you ask
      what was your friend's name?

I forgot, I say. You hear the lie,
    demand I put his picture and name
      in the piano bench, inside the purple book

with mirrors on the cover. *Is he good at math?*
　Do I have a brother? Over soup, you say
　　he should've wanted to know me,

should've told his wife—aren't you angry?
　I thought I'd given you enough of a story,
　　but under the clapboard a vine's been growing,

a prying wedge. I tell you now, I am angry.
　For not knowing you'd long to fill in the blank
　　with something other than a string of x's.

You have to learn to get up from the table when love is no longer being served.

—Nina Simone

Myths of Botany and Motherhood

Isa Down

It doesn't matter how you became a solo mama, the point is that you became one.

Became. Become. As in, you began to be. As in, you transformed. Metamorphosis.

You went from being movement—atoms spiraling around a central pole—to being the axis mundi, the heart, the Tree of Life. The center around which all matter swirls, now.

In botany, *adpressed* means to lie close to another organ, without fusing to it.

In motherhood, *adpressed* means to lie close to another, smaller, mewling version of yourself, sharing your all, without being physically fused (anymore, if at all).

The first time you saw him—the him that made life with you—you felt pulled to him, atoms realigning. You lay adpressed with him, too, lying as close to another breathing, human organ as possible without fusing to him. But fusion does not need to occur for life to affix itself, to take root. It did not matter how long atoms stood still—or how often or how far between were the moments you lay with limbs entwined—for life was planted there, in the depths of your fertile earth.

Before long, your body fed another life through the arborescent branches of the placental organ. Cells composed spines, unfurled fingers to the rhythm of your heartbeat. The whooshing of blood and muscle arranged lullabies in the womb.

The first time you held him—the him that you call child, sweet one, little love—was when he came earthbound in the sticky heat of summer. Your little water breather left his aquatic home to enter this arid landscape. You became a nectary, milk-like syrup dripping, sweet and sticky, down your child's chin.

You are the center now, life giver.

This motherhood, it is a fecund experience, oozing drops of golden light, as of honey, with each grasp of your flesh, or hair, or breath, from your tiny one. Your cells humming with life as a beehive filled to the sticky brim with honeycomb.

But it wasn't the same for him—the him that you made life with. There was no golden light seeping from his pores. The universe did not realign around him. So, however the story goes, the father left. Stripped himself off of the family unit, like the sloughing of skin, or the shedding of bark.

You were weakened, gasping as when an unexpected gust of wind meets your face or from a blow to your gut. Tremulous cracks appeared where he broke away too fast, was fused too tightly, his absence leaving nothing more than moments culled from countless breathless starts.

You were exposed. You faltered, but you remained upright, steadfast.

You can bow to the wind and not break. You are the axis mundi, after all, you remind yourself—tall and sturdy, your roots must dig deep. As though you have a choice.

But a strong root system does not make you infallible. The cracks that the father left widened with the added weight of this new, squirming life. Perhaps your tears saturated the earth too deeply, your roots wavering in the trembling mud. You felt raw: "I am too fragile now," you murmured in the night to no one in particular.

The smallest breeze could break you open.

Lawyers and arguments and anxiety and depression and the vast unknown were too much, as atoms and cells and life and breathing and cries and the glistening gossamer strings of white milk whirled past you. This is what loss and happiness and fear and strength feels like.

Maybe if you hold your little one closer, it will be enough to protect you both: enough to provide shelter.

Enough.

Fear grips you stronger than you can grip the earth. You feel defeated; the sweet honey dripping from your life thickens, stagnates. You feel battered from all directions, as though atop a cliff, strong winds veiling your face, making it hard to breathe. Your roots become saturated, tenuous, and you feel the only thing holding you to this solid earth are noxious weeds clambering up your limbs, suffocating you.

But there is another here, now, with you: a faint cry from your babe, carried to you on gusts of chaos, beckons you. You are awakened.

And this madness emboldens you. And so you become the eye of the storm as chaos creates seismic shifts around you.

You lift your drooping, nodding head and breathe fire. This turmoil has put weight in your bones, motherhood has broadened the curve of your hip, and you have a solid foundation from which to soar, emboldened. You send out new shoots, your boundary in constant shift as new root after new root emerges from your chaotic structure. You are fierce. You are mama.

This is the thing that awakens you in the night and whispers encouragement through exhaustion, pushes you past your breaking point. It is beautiful and fecund and abundant. It is laughter and tears and joy and shame and strength and struggles. It is power.

You rise to meet this messy life: motherhood.

Gravity

Kim Addonizio

Carrying my daughter to bed
I remember how light she once was,
no more than a husk in my arms.
There was a time I could not put her down,
so frantic was her crying if I tried
to pry her from me, so I held her
for hours at night, walking up and down the hall,
willing her to fall asleep. She'd grow quiet,
pressed against me, her small being alert
to each sound, the tension in my arms, she'd take
my nipple and gaze up at me,
blinking back fatigue she'd fight whatever terror
waited beyond my body in her dark crib. Now
that she's so heavy I stagger beneath her,
she slips easily from me, down
into her own dreaming. I stand over her bed,
fixed there like a second, dimmer star,
though the stars are not fixed: someone
once carried the weight of my life.

The Nervous Hospital

Mary Karr

The intake nurse brings me back a steaming mug of tea, taking from her drawer packets of honey and sugar and little red plastic stirring sticks, and the small civility of this makes me want to run out the door. I'm in a state of mind that can only be described as feral.

She settles back to typing the form, asking, You and your husband are at the same address?

We go back and forth, I say. We've been separated less than a month.

I've refused to call my husband so far, though my therapist rang him before she arranged for me to get admitted. The mere sound of Warren's voice would slam down on me a sledgehammer of guilt at leaving him to care for Dev solo.

After fourteen hours sacked out in the bin, I wake to find my mouth glued together. Beside my bed are a pair of green foam slippers embossed with smiley faces, which design seems a grotesque mistake on somebody's part. I step right into them. I tie on the striped robe they'd given me, then stump out to accept whatever I've signed up for.

At the nurses' station, I'm handed a paper cup with another double dose of antidepressants to toss down.

In the dayroom, I find a game show blaring at two women. One's a large woman holding a teddy bear missing both eyes. The other's fortyish, with a flapper's curly bob and a small, muscular frame.

I'm Tina, she says, manic-depressive.

I'm Mary, I say, depressive-depressive.

On TV, the correct door has been chosen by a woman who bounces up and down and claps at a new bedroom set.

Tina's dressed in bike shorts and a lime-green striped athletic jersey with the Italian flag on the sleeve. She says to the other lady, Do you want to tell Mary your name?

I'm Dimples, she says in a little girl voice. She's white as parchment, with soft flesh that spills as if poured from her sleeves and shorts legs.

On TV, a horn honks. The audience sighs with disappointment. Tell her your bear's name, too, Tina prompts. But Dimples just covers her face with the eyeless animal and falls quiet.

We're supposed to engage her, but she's no Dale Carnegie. Multiple personality disorder. Tina says, Do you work out?

This starts me crying.

For the first few weeks, I turn into a regular waterworks. In my family, we claim to cry at card tricks, but with no card tricks in sight, I sob my guts out. Anybody who'll listen to my sorrows gets an earful, and since each shift features a nurse ordained to hear me out—Mary, preeminently—at least twice a day, I boohoo my head off. Plus group therapy. Plus a shrink they assign me three times a week. Which makes those first days dissolve together into a kind of steam-room fog I sit red-faced in the middle of, blowing my nose.

I mostly cry about the pain I know I'm causing Dev by going inpatient. And I sob about his dad, whose tenderness for me has perhaps been killed off by my small black heart. And I wail in abject terror that—now I'm not only an alcoholic but also a lunatic—Warren will divorce me and take Dev.

When Warren comes in wearing khaki shorts and a kind, owlish expression to meet with the social worker and me, saying he wants to work on loving each other better, I blubber with hope at our prospects. I swear forever to love him till death, and while there's still a blank between us, I mean it.

(Here, I mistrust my memory, which holds no long talk between us of the type I'd have insisted on if our roles were reversed.)

He and Dev come every afternoon to eat dinner with me in a private room. I cry before they arrive, then weep when they stride out.

That afternoon, when Warren and Dev show up, I feel a rush of delight just seeing them. Warren opens the stairwell door with one hand so Dev can slide past him, and the instant stays haloed in gold, for it's my first conscious memory of something solidly good. Though their afternoon visit is always the day's highlight, it routinely sends a volcano of guilt up my middle, since Dev always steps onto the ward with such hesitance, a posture almost soldierly in its wary vigilance. (Even now, from a distance of eighteen years, he remembers how scary the place was.)

Dev was born into a bold certainty of feeling. About nearly everything, he held convictions. As a newborn, he had the appetite of a jackal. As a toddler, once faced with a tea service at my in-laws, he'd stuck his fist in the sugar bowl and upended it, sugar spraying all over as Mrs. Whitbread hissed that no other child in that house had ever interfered with a tea. While other toddlers had winced at new food, he had a taste for sashimi, for steak tartare with raw onion and egg yolk. He approached stray dogs with his arms open, ran full speed into waves.

Yet he was all sensibility. (In a few years, I'd see Dev stand once for a long time before two Cubist paintings—one Braque and one

Picasso—announcing, I know I'm supposed to like the Picasso more, but this one's stronger. And so it had been.) He was sturdily resolute in all his tastes.

That day in the hospital, Dev comes in dressed in a Hawaiian print shirt, looking like a miniature Miami dope dealer, and wary that way, as if expecting to find machine guns in the hands of rival gang members as he slides under Warren's arm.

But instead of my usual stab of concern or guilt, I see this as a single instant in his life amid a zillion other instants with attendant feelings—love, curiosity, desire. His curls are damp around the edges from the heat. I heave him up and inhale an odor of wet earth in his hair, and he plants a dry kiss on my cheek. I let him down and greet Warren, balancing a coffee holder with two steaming cups and a crumpled pastry bag. His white shirt, rolled up at the wrists, shows the lineaments of his brown forearms. He holds the coffee to one side, bending so I can kiss him, and in his preoccupied expression is infinite gentleness. I place my lips on his square jaw and taste the living salt of him.

In the kitchen a few minutes later, the first creamy sip of strong coffee gives me a distinct flood of pleasure. I remember a few similar instants when I first quit drinking.

Nothing has changed, really. The uncertainty of my marriage is still there. But some equanimity exists, as if some level in my chest has ceased its endless teetering and found its balance point.

Stay afraid, but do it anyway. What's important is the action. You don't have to be confident. Just do it and eventually the confidence will follow.

—Carrie Fisher

What Remains

Jaimie Seaton

"What do you want to do with these?"

I look in the box and touch the cream fabric imprinted with dark green images of trees and leaves and a man in traditional Chinese dress swinging on a vine and think back to our days in Thailand. I had chosen the fabric with such care and had the bed linens custom made: a box-pleat bed skirt, two large rectangular pillows, and two pillow shams.

"These go on the king bed," I reply.

I pause, thinking of how my ex-husband, Hans, took the bed to New York the previous weekend. There is no point in saving them. I will never use them again.

"Put them in his box," I say, exhaling.

I've hired Mark, my teenage daughter's boyfriend, for this very odd summer job—helping me sort through the remnants of my marriage. It's an undertaking I've been avoiding for three years, ever since I moved with my two children from our lavish Colonial in the country to a small split-level in town. Hans had shattered our family two years earlier when he left me for another woman—who was pregnant with his child.

A simpler home with simpler furnishings allowed the kids and me a fresh start, but I hadn't been ready to let go of all the precious things I had gathered in my quest to cultivate the perfect family, or at least the image of one. So when we moved, I stacked the unused, opulent furnishings next to the boxes in the basement and did my best to forget about them.

Year after year, my children and I tossed more objects—dried flowers, the remnants of sewing projects, Halloween costumes, a new blow-up Santa—on top of the boxes, adding a fresh layer of memories to those beneath. When I descended those stairs to do laundry or get the vacuum, the boxes haunted me. No matter how perfectly I cleaned the rest of the house, anguish and disorder lay hidden in the basement—my own Dorian Grey portrait, writ large.

The previous summer, I made a half-hearted attempt to clean the basement, but could only bring myself to open boxes briefly and scribble their contents on the outside. Some had been sorted: books, my grandmother's Haviland Limoges china, photographs from high school, my children's old schoolwork. But most were labeled NEED TO SORT in large black letters. They contained sentimental reminders of a romantic courtship in South Africa, the births of our children, life as a happy family in Asia, and, finally, divorce documents.

A year later, Christine asked if I had any odd jobs for Mark to do. *This might be just what I need*, I thought: an impartial presence to force me to do what I didn't want to do; all the better that I had to pay him. Spending money on the endeavor would keep me in check: I wouldn't squander hours reliving every moment of my marriage if a meter was running.

For three days, Mark and I worked side by side, hauling boxes to the garage to make room, vacuuming cobwebs, and filling bags labeled

"Salvation Army" or "Trash" and boxes marked "Hans." We moved furniture and stood, arms crossed, surveying the space and deciding the best way to organize the things that would remain. We filled the back of my car with items not worth saving, and Mark drove them to the dump, while I remained at home on the floor lost in memory.

Sometimes my teenage kids would pitch in, and we'd all laugh, reading funny poems they'd written as young children or gushing over their primitive artwork. On the second day, while we sat sorting, I held up a soft button-down shirt with faded blue-and-white checks.

"This goes," I said.

"What is that?" Christine asked.

"This is the shirt your father wore on our first date," I replied, remembering how we drove along Jan Smuts Road in Johannesburg in his maroon mini Golf, full of butterflies and anticipation.

She reached for the shirt.

"I want that," she said.

As I handed it over, I remembered the flower ring dotted with diamonds and emeralds that I keep in my nightstand. Years after my parents' divorce, my mother gave it to me, describing how my father had surprised her with it soon after they were married. When I later asked my father about the ring, he got a wistful look on his face and said he noticed it in a shop window one evening after work and bought it simply because he thought it was pretty. It was such a sweet, impulsive gesture for a man who was neither. It was difficult for me to imagine the man I knew—who, when he put me to sleep as a child would inspect the bed I made that morning and, if the hospital corners weren't perfect 45-degree angles, rip off the sheets and force me to remake it—doing something so kind for my mother. The ring, and its origin, comforted me and gave me a sliver of tangible proof that my father hadn't always been a monster, that somewhere deep beneath his cruelty was a soul capable of love and youthful flights of fancy.

Hans had not torn off our sheets, but he had callously ripped our life apart. Probably more so than I, our children were left to reconcile the father they loved, who had shown them such tenderness, with the man who broke their hearts. In taking the shirt, perhaps Christine was trying to diminish her memory of my anger, seeking proof that I once loved her father so much that I would keep his old faded shirt for twenty years.

That summer with Mark, I abandoned my work and spent hours alone hunched over boxes on the concrete basement floor, kneeling on a pad I use for gardening to spare my knees. With every item sorted, I became lighter. I became obsessed with finishing the job, forcing myself to swim the channel so I could emerge on that distant shore of healing and rebirth.

When my ex-husband came up from New York for the weekend, I met him in the driveway holding the Thai bed linens in a clear plastic bag.

"These go with the king bed that you took last weekend," I said.

He looked at the linens and said nothing.

"You took that bed to her place, right?"

"Yes," he responded matter-of-factly.

"I can't imagine why the two of you want to sleep in our bed, but if you do, you may as well have the linens." I put them in his hands. "I've cleaned the basement, and you need to take all of your things to storage this weekend," I said as I walked to the house.

Later that afternoon, I watched as he and Mark loaded a U-Haul with the handmade Russian silk rug purchased on a whim in Singapore, green lamps from our master bedroom, African masks, and framed artwork. Objects collected during nearly twenty years together had become flotsam.

Over the next few days, something gnawed at me, like when you know you've forgotten something but can't remember what. Then I realized what was missing: the tape that had run mercilessly in my head, berating me, begging me to clean the basement, had ceased and had been replaced by something else—quiet joy, even triumph.

We used the extra space in the basement to set up an art room for my son. The white table on which he works is now piled high with scraps of fabric and paper, paints, bits of moss, and pieces of cardboard. As the pile grows higher, I smile, thinking of the new happy memories it contains.

My daughter is off to college now. On her last night at home, she slept in the faded blue-and-white shirt that her father wore on our first date.

It Will Look
Like a Sunset

Kelly Sundberg

"You made me hit you in the face," he said mournfully. "Now everyone is going to know."

I was twenty-six, having spent most of my twenties delaying adulthood, and he was twenty-four and enjoyed a reputation as a partier. The pregnancy was a surprise, and we married four months later.

As my belly stretched outward with the tightness of the baby, my limbs grew heavy. I napped constantly on a long hand-me-down couch, the summer heat giving me nightmares. I dreamt of a woman floating in the corner staring at me, and I woke with my heart racing. One afternoon, a hummingbird flew through the open door of the apartment to the window in the corner and beat at the glass. It was panicked, trying to turn glass into sky. I wrapped my hands around it, the hummingbird heart pulsing against my palms, then released it on the stoop.

They say that a bird in the house is an omen. It can mean pregnancy. Or death. Or both.

Eight years later, the police came to our door. When the younger one asked about my foot, I said that it didn't hurt. I told him it was no big deal, but when he asked for my driver's license, I stood up and found that I couldn't walk, that my foot was the size of a football, and it was bleeding. The bowl Caleb had shattered on it wasn't a little bowl like I had described. It was a heavy, ceramic serving bowl, and I would need to wear a soft boot for a month and get a tetanus shot, and there would always be a scar shot through the top of my foot like a red star.

In the beginning of our relationship, I slept in his cabin in the woods with no indoor plumbing. I had to pee, so I let myself out. The ground was snow-covered and cold and I didn't feel like walking to the outhouse, so I went around to the side and squatted in the moonlight. The moon turned the snow into a million stars while my gentle lover slumbered in the warmth—such happiness.

We didn't want a church wedding, but our families insisted. Faith was what made marriage sacred. Faith was what kept people together.

I had doubts about marrying him so soon. Sometimes, he would disappear for a straight week and return apologetic, smelling of alcohol. His friends gave each other looks that said they knew something I did not. One friend said jokingly, "How on earth did Caleb get you to go out with him?" Coming from a friend, the question seemed odd, but I thought it was just the way they ribbed each other.

When I met him, he charmed me. My best friend said: "You'll love Caleb. He lives in a cabin in the woods that he built by himself." A former wilderness ranger, I was attracted to ruggedness and solitude. Caleb was a writer, and he was funny. One day, he joked in bed about what our rapper names would be. I said mine would be "Awesome Possum." He improvised a rap song titled "Get in My Pouch!" I couldn't stop giggling. I had never met a man who could make me laugh like he could.

My love for him was real, and I didn't want to be a single mother.

The young policeman told Caleb, "Go to your parents. Get away for a couple of days. Just let things calm down."

The young policeman told me, "It's alright. My wife and I fight. Things get crazy. Sometimes you just need time apart."

I nodded my head in agreement, but I wanted to ask, "Do you beat your wife, too?"

Before our son turned two, we moved to Caleb's home state of West Virginia. He wanted to be closer to his family. There would be more opportunity for work there. His parents owned a rental house that they would sell to us. There were many compelling reasons for the move, but once there, he was the only friend I had. The loneliness was inescapable. This was common, I told myself. My parents had been married for over thirty years, and I don't remember my father ever having a close friend. I told myself that he was enough for me.

When the older policeman saw the swelling, the black and blue, and the toes like little sausage links, his expression turned to dismay. "That's bad. That looks broken," he said. "Ma'am, does your husband have a phone number we can reach him at? We need him to come back."

They waited outside, and I called Caleb. "I'm sorry," I said. "They are going to arrest you."

He said he already knew.

He left his phone on while they arrested him so I could listen. I didn't want to, but I couldn't stop myself. "Did she hit you?" one of the officers asked. "Because we can arrest her, too."

Caleb answered honestly. He said no.

We were together for almost two years before he was violent with me. First he pushed me against a wall. It was two more years before he hit me, and another year after that before he hit me again. It happened so slowly, then so fast.

While the older policeman arrested Caleb, the younger one waited with me for the paramedics to arrive. "Is he going to lose his job?" I asked.

"No, probably not," he said.

"Is he going to leave me?" I asked.

"You didn't do anything wrong," he said.

I wanted him to hug me so I could hide my face in the folds of his black uniform. I crumpled into the rocking chair instead.

"He's going to leave me," I said.

When our elderly neighbor developed dementia and, one night, thought a boy was hiding under her bed, Caleb stayed with her. When the child of an administrative assistant in Caleb's department needed a heart transplant, Caleb went to the assistant's house and helped him put down wood floors in his basement to create a playroom for the little boy. When my dad needed help installing new windows in the house, or mowing the lawn, or chopping wood, Caleb was always ready to help. I was so grateful to be married to someone so generous with his time, so loving.

The young policeman called for an ambulance. The EMTs looked at my foot. They didn't ask about what happened. They just told me it looked bad, that it could be broken. They asked me if I wanted to go to the emergency room, but I declined, so they instructed me to see a doctor and made me sign a waiver saying they weren't responsible if I didn't get follow-up care. And then I was alone in our home.

Two years after we moved, I started graduate school and finally made some friends, but it was hard to spend time with them. I had to lie: I shut my arm in the door. I tripped on a rug and hit my face on the table. I don't know where that bruise came from. I think I did it in my sleep. I think I'm anemic. I just bruise so easily.

Once, Caleb said to me, "You probably wish that someone would figure out where those bruises are coming from. You probably wish someone knew, so that things could change." He said it with such sadness.

After the arrest, I hobbled around in denial for a few days until a concerned friend pushed me into getting the foot examined.

I was embarrassed at the urgent care center. I told the nurse, "It's okay. He's already been arrested. I don't need anything. I'm safe," but he didn't seem to believe me. The nurse put me in a wheelchair even though I insisted I could walk, and the doctor touched and turned my foot with such care that, out of some sort of misguided impulse, I almost blurted out, "Mom!" But I was thirty-four years old, and the distance between my mother and me was punctuated by so many mountains that she couldn't have saved me.

Caleb wanted to change. He got therapy. He went to anger management. He did everything right. We were allies. Together, we were going to fix this problem.

He started taking medication shortly after our sixth anniversary.

Every time he was violent with me, he would go to a psychiatrist who increased his dosage. I thought the psychiatrist could fix him.

He wasn't supposed to drink on the medication, but he did. One night, he was in a stupor and staring at something. "What are you looking at?" I asked.

"Myself," he said. "That's me sitting in that chair." He pointed at an empty chair across the room. "That me is laughing at me." His eyes were confused, sad.

"Are you manipulating me?" I asked, worried.

"I'm not the one who manipulates you," he said. He gestured toward the chair again, his voice quickening, earnest almost. "He's the one who manipulates you. It's not me."

I was so tired. I didn't know what to say. "You should go to bed."

His eyes turned from sadness to rage. He stood up and went to the stairs, then turned back to me and said, "I hope you get chlamydia and die."

Shortly before I left him, I told a counselor that my husband was hitting me and showed her the bruises. She held me while I wept in her arms. I then told a close friend that he yelled at me and called me names, but I didn't yet tell her he was beating me.

My counselor said, "You are taking everything he says, and playing it on repeat over and over again. You have to stop the tape."

But I couldn't stop the tape. I heard over and over:

You are a fucking cunt. You are a fucking cunt. You are a fucking cunt. You are a fucking cunt. You are a fucking cunt. You are a fucking cunt. You are a fucking cunt.

And then his voice became my voice:

I am a fucking cunt.

"You can't hold the things I say when I'm mad against me," he said. "That isn't fair. Those aren't the things I mean."

At the urgent care, the doctor said, "This will take a long time to heal. It will change color over time. It will look like a sunset." As I drove home, I heard the words over and over:

It will look like a sunset. It will look like a sunset. It will look like a sunset. It will look like a sunset. It will look like a sunset. It will look like a sunset. It will look like a sunset.

I could never bring myself to leave. Instead, I was a regular at the Travelodge. I always returned home before morning, keeping the hotel key card just in case, then climbing into bed and wrapping my arms around Caleb's back. All of the usual suspects drew me back—concerns about our six-year-old, money, where we would live, and love. I still loved him. I told myself he would get better.

In sickness, and in health. Those were my vows in that little church in Idaho where we held hands while sunlight filtered through stained glass and spring lilacs bloomed outside. Caleb was sick.

He only hit me in the face once. A red bruise bloomed across my cheek, and my eye was split and oozing. Afterwards, we both sat on the bathroom floor, exhausted. "You made me hit you in the face," he said mournfully. "Now everyone is going to know."

A month or so before his arrest, I thought I was losing my hair from stress. In the shower, red strands swam in the water by my feet. Chunks were stuck to my fingers. It didn't matter. I hadn't felt pretty in years.

When I rubbed the shampoo into my scalp, the skin was tender, and I realized I wasn't losing my hair. He had ripped it out, and I hadn't even felt it.

I went into a cave when he hit me. I curled into my body like a slug, then traveled into a deep darkness where I felt nothing. I heard his voice, his fists, the blasts in my ears from the blows to the side of my head. I heard my own screaming.

Deep in that cave, it wasn't real, even as it was happening.

What was real was when we laid in bed, our son between us—my head on my husband's shoulder, his head resting on mine—and our son said, "The whole family is cuddled up."

"I'm not the type of person to hit a woman," he said. "So it must be you. You are the one who brings this out in me. I would not be like this if I was with a different woman."

The same night that Caleb pulled out my hair, he punched me in the spine with such force that my body arched back as though it had been shocked with electricity. I was jolted out of my cave. He did it again. "No," I screamed. I could not protect myself.

My only protection was the darkness—the dissociation. I hadn't felt him ripping out hair, but when he hit me in the spine, the pain was too intense. That part of my body was too vulnerable. I couldn't curl up. I couldn't wrap my arms around it.

I was present for what was happening. I stopped breathing for a moment. He paused.

It was as though he, too, felt that I was present, and he stopped. I couldn't have been human to him in those moments.

He never raped me, so there's that.

I left him two days after he was arrested, but I wasn't ready. I still wasn't ready.

We were one of those couples that others liked to be around. We laughed a lot, respected each other, and supported each others' work. We loved the same things: cooking Thai food, impromptu dance parties in the living room, *Friday Night Lights* marathons. We always found time for date nights. We vacationed in Greece, New York City, and Glacier National Park. We emailed each other silly videos during the day when we were at work. He phoned me from the car, five minutes after leaving the house, just to talk.

The day that I left him, I called Rebecca, a kind and accepting friend whom I knew would help. It wasn't an easy call to make.

She lived with her partner, and they let my son and me stay with them for a month until we had our own place. She and I had only known each other for a little over a year. I told her about the beatings, how Caleb broke my phone when I tried to call for help, how he pulled me out from underneath the bed by my ankles, how I hid shaking in the closet while he raged, how he always found me, how there was no safe place for me.

When I saw the fear in her eyes, I understood the magnitude of what was happening.

Of everyone I had dated, he was the gentlest. I loved his soft hands, his embraces, his kind heart.

He wrote me love letters, rubbed my feet, took me out to lunch, got up first in the mornings with our son, so that I could sleep in. He took care of me. He was more often kind to me than unkind.

Sometimes, when I'm cooking dinner by myself, I can feel the way he would lay his head on my shoulder while I stirred a pot, the way he would turn me around and kiss me, tell me how much he loved my cooking, how beautiful I was, how lucky he was.

On Thanksgiving Day, Caleb took our son to his family's annual Thanksgiving dinner. While they ate turkey and dressing around the oak table I had eaten at so many times before, I returned to my home with Rebecca and threw as many things as I could fit into laundry baskets, then stuffed them into the backseat of my car. I packed my son's Legos, enough blankets for us to sleep on the floor, and my work clothes, but I left behind anything sentimental. Our wedding photo was on a table, the glass broken. I had thrown it on the ground.

After packing, Rebecca and I ate at a Chinese buffet attached to a casino because it was the only place open in three counties. The future loomed before me like a buffet full of hungry, lonely people.

My favorite photo of Caleb and me is a self-portrait taken on a beach at Ecola State Park on the Oregon Coast. We had hiked down a steep trail, stopping to lunch on smoked salmon and bagels, and ended up on a beach. The tide was low, and sand dollars dotted the shore. We scooped them up like prizes. We ran into the surf. We hugged. In the photo, we are both smiling, our heads pressed together.

When I look at that photo now, I wonder, "Where are those people? Where did they go?"

Just to the right of us was a cave. I had wanted to go in it, but the tide was coming in, and I was afraid of getting trapped and drowning.

Six months after I left Caleb, I went home to Idaho for the summer. After that, I was moving to another state. It was over. The counselor at the domestic violence shelter was proud of me. So many women never get out. I didn't feel proud. I didn't want to get out. I wanted to keep dancing with Caleb, keep sending funny emails to each other, keep cuddling with our son between us.

There are days when I still wish that he would beg me to take him back, promise to change, actually change. This will never happen. Even if he never hit me again, my body will always remember that fist on my back.

In Idaho, the state where Caleb and I met, where we had our son, I drove the sunbaked streets. There was the apartment where Caleb sat next to me on the couch, nervously wiped his hand across his forehead, and said in a halting voice, "Kelly, I want to marry you."

There was the house where our baby slept in a basket by the bed. When he cried, I nursed him while Caleb draped his arm around my waist, nuzzling his head into my hair.

There was the riverside trail where we pushed the stroller and fantasized over which fancy house we would buy if we ever had any money, where our toddler threw sticks into the river, where Caleb scooped him up and held him upside down while we all giggled.

There was the river where, in winter, our dog slid out onto the ice and into the cold water. Caleb stretched out on the ice and reached his hands out to our dog while I watched terrified. "I can't lose you both," I screamed.

I wondered if it would have happened if we had stayed in Idaho.

But then there was the house where he first pushed me up against a wall, where he backed me into the corner, where he threw our baby's bouncer. The neighbor watched worried from her stoop while he put the broken pieces in the trash can on the curb, and I cried in the window.

The same house where my mother took me into the backyard and said, "Listen to me. I have friends who have left their husbands. I have seen it on the other side. It is not better on the other side. Try hard. Try hard before you give up."

I tried so hard.

I left my husband but kept photos of my battered self. I kept them in my purse, so I would never forget or become weak.

—Lisa Richardson

Cicadas

Rachel Jamison Webster

The neighbors give me gin and olives
and I slosh it all over my Levis.
I feel like a real adult, I say and laugh
wondering when that will happen,
when my life will solidify around me
like a carapace made of the concentrated
proteins of my choices. The girls
are rollerblading along the sidewalk
and find three cicada shells that they stick
onto their t-shirts. The boldest girl—
bold because she's overlooked—dares
herself to bite the legs off one
and chews. *What does it taste like?* I ask.
I don't think it tastes like anything,
she says, considering, then looks
me in the eye and asks if I'm surprised.

No, I say, *I'm just wondering what your life*
will be like if you're already this unafraid.
She is nine and taller on her rollerblades.
I know she sees the ancient and alien
and wants to take it into her body, alchemize it
until she holds what it knows,
until she's solved the crouch and claw
that people call *other*. I don't say that
I'm her again, skating off into wind,
and also this adult drinking gin
on the lawn with her parents.
Her father is talking about the nutritional
concentration in insects—how we
should harness it to solve world starvation—
and her mother is recalling their wedding
night at the tacky hotel in the Poconos,
how they got so hungry they just ordered
a pizza. I can't believe I'm alone again
like someone without a complete set of skin.
When I sat down on the blanket,
I found a single wing, disembodied,
filigreed and paned as leaded glass.
It was shaped for slicing the air, hefting
the armored body on its drifts.
I plucked up its little glinting chip,
and stuck it behind my ear,
because its memory of flight
seems to me worth protecting,
seems the most important thing.

My Books on Divorce

Amy Poehler

I understand why people read so many books on divorce. When you are a person going through a divorce you feel incredibly alone, yet you are constantly reminded by society of how frequently divorce happens and how common it has become. You aren't allowed to feel special, but no one understands the specific ways you are in pain. Imagine spreading everything you care about on a blanket and then tossing the whole thing up in the air. The process of divorce is about loading up that blanket, throwing it up, watching it all spin, and worrying what stuff will break when it lands. It's no wonder we want to find answers and comfort.

I don't want to talk about my divorce because it is too sad and too personal. I also don't like people knowing my shit. I will say a few things. I am proud of how my ex-husband, Will, and I have been taking care of our children; I am beyond grateful he is their father; and I don't think a ten-year marriage constitutes failure. That being said, getting a divorce really sucks. But as a dear friend has noted, "divorce is always good news because no good marriage has ever ended in divorce."

Any painful experience makes you see things differently. It also reminds you of the simple truths that we purposely forget every day or else we would never get out of bed. Things like, nothing lasts forever and relationships can end. The best that can happen is you learn a little more about what you can handle and you stay soft through the pain. Perhaps you feel a little wiser. Maybe your experience can be of help to others. With that in mind, here are some titles for a series of divorce books I would like to pitch to you and my editors for future discussion. After review, I realize that all of my books have exclamation points at the end of their titles, but I think people want exclamation points in the titles of their books, and I don't think I am wrong!!!!

1.
I WANT A DIVORCE! SEE YOU TOMORROW!

If you have small children you will understand this book. This book deals with the fact that most people who divorce with small children still need to see each other every day. Any good parent will try to put their children's needs first, and so this book will help teach you how to have a knock-down, drag-out fight and still attend a kid's birthday party together on the same day. Are you in your early twenties and recently broke up with someone over Skype? This book is not for you. Have you successfully avoided your ex for over six months except for a close call at your friend's art opening? This book is not for you. Have you heard secondhand that your ex is building houses for Habitat for Humanity and you rolled your eyes at how fucking phony the whole thing sounded and then sighed because you don't miss him but you liked playing with his dog? This book is not for you. This book is for the people who have to work together or live together or co-parent together while going through a divorce.

Chapters include:

- *FAKE SMILING*
- *HOW IMPORTANT IS THE LAST WORD?*
- *PHONE CALLS ON THE WAY HOME FROM THERAPY*
- *EVERYONE NEEDS TO STOP BUYING TOYS*

2.

GET OVER IT! (BUT NOT TOO FAST!)

When you are going through the trauma and drama of divorce, you learn who your real friends are. They guide you and take care of you and save you from your darkest days. The problem is, you also have to talk to other people about this bullshit, and it's often people you don't care about or like. Usually these people are very interested at first and then have to go back to their own lives and want you to do the same. This book is here to remind you that even though you are in pain and still in transition, everyone else has moved on and is a little tired of your situation. This book will remind you that unless you and your ex-spouse got into a juicy fight or there are some new boyfriends and girlfriends in the mix, most people don't want to talk about it anymore. This book will also teach you how you need to move on, but not too fast. It will remind you that you are allowed to be upset, but for god's sake please keep it together. You need to seem sad at just the right times or else other people will think you're weird. You also need to be able to act normal at the parties they invite you to.

Chapters include:

- *SHE DOESN'T CRY ENOUGH*
- *HE SEEMS GAY TO ME*
- *THIS WON'T GET YOU OUT OF A SPEEDING TICKET*

- *I'M SORRY TO INTERRUPT, BUT WHEN DO YOU THINK YOU WILL BE OVER IT?*

3.

DIVORCE: TEN WAYS TO NOT CATCH IT!

Divorce is contagious! Haven't you heard? It's like cancer but worse because no one really feels that bad for you. This book will teach you how to discuss your divorce with your currently married friends. Some married couples get freaked out when you talk about your divorce and like to tell you how they aren't going to get one. Usually they point to their hard work through therapy, their fear of being alone, or their total acceptance of a dead marriage devoid of sex and love. This book will help you not strangle them when they both stand in front of you and talk about how great their relationship continues to be. This book will also help you deal with the divorce voyeur, the friend who wants to hear every detail and live vicariously through your experience. This book will point to ways you can talk about your divorce without feeling like it's a fancy fur coat that people like to try on but then throw back at you in disgust because they would never wear something so vile. This book contains illustrations of happy couples looking at you with pity, and some weird aphorisms that intimate it's somehow easier to get divorced than to stay in an unhappy marriage.

Chapters include:

- *DIVORCE IS NOT AN OPTION FOR ME, BUT I AM HAPPY FOR YOU*
- *C'MON, WHO HASN'T CHEATED?*
- *I JUST COULDN'T DO THAT TO MY KIDS*
- *MAYBE YOU GUYS JUST NEED TO GO TO OJAI FOR A WEEKEND*

4.
HEY, LADY, I DON'T WANT TO FUCK YOUR HUSBAND!
Newly divorced and attending a wedding for the first time alone?
This book is for you! Inside you will find ways to deal with the strange
stares and drunk accusations that come along with not having a date.
You will find tips on how to gently break it to women that you don't
want to fuck their flabby baby-faced husbands. You will find pointers
on how to deflect advances made by their husbands in full view of the
wives so you don't have to get involved in other people's weird relationship shit. You will read about the experiences of other men and
women who bravely attended events without a plus-one and came out
alive. Check out our special section on what to do when friends try to
awkwardly set you up, and our newly added bonus chapter dedicated
to those who want to be gay for a weekend.

Chapters include:

- *NO ONE AS GREAT AS YOU SHOULD BE SINGLE*
- *IS IT HARD TO BE AT A WEDDING?*
- *YOU'VE NEVER LOOKED BETTER*
- *HAVE YOU SEEN MARK ANYWHERE? I CAN'T
  FIND HIM*

5.
GOD IS IN THE DETAILS!
This book will help you navigate all the intimate details that people
want to know and, frankly, have a right to know. This includes how
did you break up and where are you living now and who wanted it
more and how long did you know and what is going on with the kids
and how did you tell the kids and was it sad and is he mad and are you
sad and does everyone know and who have you told and who can I tell

and when will you make an announcement and does Margaret know and is it okay for me to call her and what's going on with the house and who is getting the money and how much money is it, exactly, and does Margaret know because I feel like she needs to hear it from me and do you have a boyfriend and does he have a girlfriend and what are their names and how much do they weigh and are weekends lonely and are you happier and do you think you will ever get married again and are you going to have more kids and could you just tell me exactly every detail from the beginning especially the bad stuff?

6.
THE HOLIDAYS ARE RUINED!
This book is one page long and just contains that one sentence.

My hope is these manuals will help you navigate such a supremely shitty time. I promise you, someday happy couples won't make you cry anymore. Someday you may be in one again. Someday you will wake up feeling 51 percent happy and slowly, molecule by molecule, you will feel like yourself again. Or you will lose your mind and turn into a crazy person. Either way, let's just hope you avoided tattoos, because most are pretty stupid anyway.

Today, I Am Mostly Crying

Claire Gillespie

I wasn't expecting to spend today in tears. After all, I've gotten what I want. After four years of us living separate lives, I finally filed for divorce. Today, my husband will be served with the papers.

I cry watching my daughter eat breakfast. She is so like him. She has his small nose and expressive eyes, his skin tone and his calf muscles. Sleepily chewing her cereal, a strand of her hair floating in the milk, she has no idea what is happening today.

I cry when my son grabs me in an unexpected hug. He is so like me. He has my long limbs and large mouth. He, too, has no idea what is happening today.

At six and eight years old, perhaps it doesn't matter that they don't know. What they do know is what kind of family we are. We are different from some, similar to others. They know our marriage ended a long time ago. To them, divorce paperwork is an unnecessary part of the story. But for us, it is more than necessary. We must close this chapter to be able to begin the next one.

I think of our children as babies, and I cry again: my son, taut as a muscle, with huge blue eyes set to break a million hearts; my daughter, tiny, with skin that smelled of summer, her hands in permanent fists, ready to take on the world. My husband was—is—such a good father to them, the perfect combination of loyal protector and unpredictable court jester.

"Yin and yang," he used to say about us, and for a few years, we both believed that was a good thing.

We barely knew each other before we were staring down the barrel of a positive pregnancy test, then staring at each other and deciding in that moment to hope for the best. Maybe if our son hadn't arrived so unexpectedly, our relationship would have fizzled out like so many twenty-somethings' liaisons do. But he did arrive, and we are thankful for that.

I cry when I think of our wedding day. Our son was there—eighteen months old, clingy, oblivious. We danced and laughed and stole a moment, just us, away from the crowd, to reaffirm the promises of a life together we weren't sure we would be able to keep. We were never wonderful together, but it was a wonderful day.

He calls me to tell me the divorce papers have arrived. "I've been served," he chuckles. "I'm not sure what to do," he says, and he sounds very young. My eyes well up again. "You don't need to do anything," I tell him. We both know he will not contest this; we both know it is for the best. We simply have to wait for a judge we will never meet to decide that, yes, we are allowed to legally end our marriage.

I have never been divorced before, so I don't know how a day like this is supposed to feel. I am unwavering, relieved, and optimistic about my future as a divorced woman in her thirties. Yet I am also grieving the loss of our marriage. There will be no champagne corks popping on this occasion, no divorce parties in this house.

I take the children to the park, and I cry behind large sunglasses. I remember our first date, when lunch became drinks, then dinner, then ridiculous chatter in a smoky bar. I had large sunglasses on that day, too. I went to the bathroom and returned to find him wearing them. "You look like an ant," I said, before we kissed.

He collects the kids for the weekend, and it's business as usual. He hands me a bag of their clothes, not clean, but I don't mind. I tell him he looks tired. "Daddy's not sleeping," says our daughter.

"Only because I'm missing you so much," he replies.

He is talking to her, not me.

I hold it together until they leave, then I press my ear to the front door to hear their chatter, staying like that until I can hear only silence. And then I cry. Oh, how I cry.

We didn't have the marriage we hoped we would have, but we do have a friendship, and we will be tied forever by the children who breathe life into our souls. Our marriage was far from a failure.

Later, I drive to the supermarket for cat food and beer. The first person I see is him. Standing at the checkout, he catches my eye and grins and waves. I smile. I see my son's blonde head bobbing by his side. I think about going over, and do an awkward, indecisive dance with my shopping cart, but I don't. This is his time with our children. They will have dinner and play games and sleep in their bedroom at Daddy's house. I will drive home from the supermarket, crying. Not because I don't want a divorce, but because I do.

Chapter Six:
Isn't It Romantic?

I go to bed wearing a very baggy one-piece cheetah suit, because it makes my son laugh. My sexy lingerie has been locked in a drawer for a while!

—Sandra Bullock

Size Queen

Evie Peck

I used to be really good at dating.

Let me rephrase that—I used to have lots of dates and all of them were horrible and on some of them, I had sex.

After becoming a solo mom, I didn't think about dating until a handsome dad at my son's school got divorced. We both had kids, we were both forty-nine, and now we were both single. For months, I thought we were flirting, and I was sure a romantic relationship would develop. Then one day he confided in me that he'd started sleeping with a woman he *really liked*, who happened to be twenty-eight.

I went through the stages of rejection: anger, denial, disgust, hunger, Botox brochures. Then I downloaded the Tinder app and started swiping right on men under thirty-two. Yes, *I too* could date people who were young enough to be my child. I only had a few dating deal breakers: conservative politics, mention of 420 in the bio, the occupation *Sales Manager*, infinity scarves, and for some reason, the name Brian. Also, any guy named Christian or who says he "loves the outdoors," because I'm Jewish.

One Sunday morning at 8 a.m. I brought my six-year-old son to the park for his baseball game. I sat in the bleachers wearing my big sun hat and took out my phone. I'd gotten three messages on Tinder. I put on my reading glasses, which I like to call *close-ups* because calling them "cheaters" or "readers" makes me feel like a granny, which I guess, numerically, I could be.

First, there was thirty-two year old Ben. In his bio, he had a picture of himself cooking and asked women to be respectful and classy. Ben wrote, "Hey, I really want to meet you. I love older women. I'm actually twenty-three."

No. I couldn't do twenty-three.

"Sorry," I wrote to Ben. "You're too young."

"Age is just a number," Ben wrote back.

I agreed, but I've got to draw the line somewhere. Children need boundaries.

A guy named Eddie wrote "Hi," so I wrote "Hi," and that ended that conversation.

Then, thirty-two-year-old Jeff wrote, "What are you looking for?" Still stinging from unrequited love over that age-appropriate divorced dad, I replied, "I'm looking for something fun and not too serious. But not a one-night stand."

"Mom," my son ran up to me, red cheeked. "Can I have my water?"

I put the phone down guiltily and said, "You're doing great out there." I hadn't seen a thing. I handed him his water, and he ran off.

"Do you like tequila and nakedness?" Jeff wrote.

The sun was shining a little too brightly for me to see my phone screen with clarity. Was he cute? Were his pictures dark for a reason? I removed my close-ups and wiped them on my T-shirt; they were from the ninety-nine-cent store and always seemed a little blurry.

"Are you a *Size Queen* by any chance?" Jeff wrote.

A size queen? What? Like queen-sized? Like L'eggs-pantyhose-in-the-egg-queen-sized? Or a queen-sized mattress?

I looked it up on urban dictionary as a baseball hummed in the background. *Size Queen* seemed to mean a woman or gay man who liked large penises.

"Do I *only* like big penises?" I wrote. I was becoming a little codependent with Jeff. Clearly he had a micro or else why would he bring it up so soon?

"Um, yeah, that's what I'm asking, I guess."

I sighed. I wasn't sure I wanted to start something with a micro. Clearly, Jeff had issues. I looked up and waved to my son in the field. He didn't see me.

"I just have a type," Jeff wrote. "I usually go for Size Queens. I love Size Queens. So . . . Are you a Size Queen?"

I hated the term *Size Queen*. I wanted him to stop writing it.

A minute later Jeff wrote, "??"

"Well, I don't like a dick so big that I'm gagging . . ." It was weird sexting at my son's game, but I was snack mom today, so I'd redeem myself later. I peeked up in time to see my son up to bat, wondering what was happening to our youth these days. *Size Queen?* Did Jeff mean *thick*, like a Hebrew National salami? Those things are delicious. Or was he talking *long*, like the twelve-ounce sunscreen spray bottle I had in my bag? I imagined shoving it in my vagina. It wasn't sexy. I thought of a few really good penises from my past. The biggest penis I was with never actually got to penetration. That guy begged off because he said he was *too nervous*. That had to be a lie, right?

"Mom, can I have my Gatorade now?"

I make my son drink most of his water before he switches to Gatorade, so he shook his empty water thermos at me to prove it. I handed him his sports drink in berry frost flavor. "You're playing so well!" I shouted as he ran back. I mean, I'm sure he was.

If only I could see Jeff's profile photos better. I hunched over and cupped my hands around the screen to block the sun's glare. I guess he was cute-ish. I just couldn't tell.

"Are your favorite ones big?" Jeff wrote.

I wanted to stop chatting about Jeff's pecker. But it was going so well—he seemed so into me.

"Are you really *that* huge?" I wrote.

"Yes."

Was I annoyed or titillated?

I started laying down juice boxes, making sure each one had its straw still attached. I separated each string cheese and opened the granola bars box. I wrote back to Jeff. "It's more about liking the guy. But if it's so big it doesn't fit . . . I don't know. I've never experienced that."

"Let's hang," Jeff wrote back, quickly.

I was losing interest with every exchange.

"Can I show you what I'm working with?"

He obviously meant a dick pic. I appreciated him asking first.

"No, thank you," I wrote back. I had to end this. "I'm at my son's baseball game so I'd better go." That, I decided, should kill the mood, thinking thirty-two was too young for me. My new cut off should be thirty-five.

"Can we FaceTime?" well-endowed Jeff wrote as the children ran off the field to grab their juice boxes. I understood why he liked me; I'd just spent the last forty-five minutes chatting about his huge member. To me it had been clinical; to him, it had been foreplay.

"Sorry, can't chat anymore. My son just threw up," I lied. My mom always said that vomiting was the only excuse that wouldn't get questioned. It didn't work for Jeff.

"Later then?" he wrote. And after few minutes, "?" then, "?????"

He didn't even ask me how my son was feeling.

I put my phone away and handed out snacks to the team.

I think maybe phone-dating isn't my scene. The swiping part is just so much fun, like playing the slots in Vegas. But with three cherries lined up in a row, I broke even and walked away.

My son ran over to me, upper lip stained baby blue with sports drink. He waved a granola bar at me. "You got the kind I like this time. Thanks for remembering," he said.

Jackpot.

All Manner of
Obscene Things

_____

Kim Addonizio

I go into the kitchen to take a couple of hits off a joint by the open window, blowing the smoke into the salt-scented air. It's where my boyfriend often stands because it's the only place in the house I'll let him smoke his Camel Lights. It's also the place where you can see the Pacific Ocean, down the hill less than a mile away. I wave the smoke toward the ocean and hurry back to our bedroom before my teenage daughter can come out of hers and catch me.

I've been watching TV for five minutes when Aya walks into my bedroom and says, "Mom, are you stoned?"

"No," I say, but she can tell. "So?" I say.

She shrugs and walks out. I'm always doing something wrong. The latest wrong thing is cheating on my boyfriend with my second ex-husband, whom Aya justifiably hates. When they first met, she didn't like him much. She already had a father, my first ex-husband, and didn't see the need of a second one hanging around us. Then he won her over. I have a picture to prove it, from a day we visited my father's grave. My second husband leans against the car door, his arm around Aya as she leans into him, a tiny eight-year-old with a blaze of blonde hair. I have another photo from that day, too, that he took without my knowing it. I'm on my knees beside the grave and a jar of wildflowers. Aya is hugging me, her face against my shoulder.

Then he left us, and I did a lot of crying and drinking. Aya loves my current boyfriend, and so do I, but I'm leaving him. I've been looking for an apartment. I can't afford anything as nice as this house we've been renting, with its high ceilings and cheerful orange walls. When Aya was in junior high, she and I shared a one-bedroom apartment; she had the bedroom, and I had a futon in the living room. Now that she's in high school we're going to need something bigger, but all the places in my price range are small and ugly.

We meet on Mondays, the ex-husband and I. We hold each other's hand in restaurants and can't let go. We kiss in his car at stop signs until another car comes up and the driver leans hard on his horn. We make love in his van, and in his flat, on the couch that smells faintly of the mice that live in it. I am too much in love to fully register the mice. By the time I do, we will be moving together to a small house in Oakland. Eventually he will borrow a large sum of money from me without my knowing it, and when I find out, that will be that. But for now, we are soul mates. We believe in our love as fervently as crazed zealots believe that by standing on an overturned crate and screaming at a busy intersection, they are bringing the word of God to the infidels.

I am deliriously happy, and I am hurting everyone.

Origami Wishes

Akesha Baron

I'm just fine right here,
being the single mother who
hangs a pale green Spanish shawl
in the kitchen window, roses in the lace.

Here with gratitude for hands,
some of which loved me well,
others that wished to
but hesitated
as if my body were foreign soil;
the hands that will one day
find their way here and
be just fine with all of it—
the child who shares my bed,
the chaos a day can turn out,
my simplistic cooking.

Today when I made my bed I arranged
the old aqua wool blanket on top
like an origami shape, peaks and folds:

Here is where I expect you to land,
on top this wool paper airplane.

Your hand will curl around the old
brass knob, its ornate design.

The weight of that wish, in my hand,
cannot be measured.

Date a woman with children only if you are ready to man up, because it's a position that comes with responsibility.

—Taraji P. Henson

How My Daughter Taught Me to Trust Again

Rachel Sarah

Leaning over the counter, my daughter ordered the same meal she always had at our favorite taqueria: a quesadilla, no salsa, no sour cream. I wasn't sure what I wanted to eat. But that wasn't all I was uncertain about.

I'd thought that bringing my eight-year-old to a familiar place to meet my new boyfriend was a good idea. But now I felt awkward. "She's going to be shy," I'd warned Chris the night before.

My daughter followed me to a table and slid into the chair next to me, our elbows touching. She grabbed a tortilla chip and crunched into it, looking straight at Chris. "Have you seen *Nacho Libre*?" she asked, referring to the Jack Black movie.

"Seen it? I own it," he said with a big grin.

"You do?" She jumped out of her seat. "Can I come over and watch it?" I guess I'd been wrong about shy.

After dinner, we all walked back to my car, making plans for our Jack Black movie night. "Thank you," I whispered, wanting to kiss Chris but instead taking a step back as my daughter wrapped her thin arms around him.

"See you soon," she said. I was silent as we drove to our apartment, just the two of us, the way it had always been. When my daughter was a baby, her father had left the country to start a new life, and I'd been a solo mom since. I wasn't going to let another man hurt me—or her.

At home I climbed into my daughter's bed, as I did every night. First, I waited for her to rearrange her pillows—the firm one, followed by the mushy ones. When she was ready, she laid her head down. It was time for us to talk about her day, something we've done since she was a baby. Without fail, dusk transformed her into an orator.

In the glow of her nightlight, she told me about school, her hands making shadows on the wall. Although she said nothing about Chris, I couldn't stop thinking about him. How would I know that he wouldn't bail on us, like my ex did?

Two weeks later, my daughter and her girlfriend were lining up dolls on our deck for a tea party when Chris biked over.

My daughter ran to him as he pulled out a bag. "Madeleines!" she shrieked. "Thank you! They're my favorite!" Chris was beaming.

Then she requested he join them. "Sit down!" she ordered Chris, pointing to the cloth on the ground, as it billowed in the wind.

Chris obeyed, slipping off his hard clip-on cycling shoes so they wouldn't tear the fabric.

My daughter's friend bent over and whispered, "Play something else?" But my daughter shook her head and turned to Chris, grinning. "Want some tea?"

I crouched down to join too. "Not you, Mama!" She crossed her arms over her chest.

Chris sipped the lukewarm tea and leaned close to my daughter. "Thank you."

Watching this scene unfold, I wasn't taken so much by the fact that my daughter had invited my boyfriend, in his biking spandex, to her tea party. It was that he wanted to be there.

I'd lost count of how many of my daughter's birthdays had passed now without a word from her father. Clearly, my daughter was already enamored of Chris' generosity, charm, and DVD collection. Why couldn't I open up to his love, the way she did?

After tea, my daughter jumped up. "I want to show you my room," she said, clasping Chris' hand. He stood and followed her inside.

If only I had the assurance to allow him in like that. Every day Chris sent me emails that said things like, "I adore you beyond belief." Yet the doubts lingered. As I leaned on the doorframe, that mistrustful voice whispered, "Is he for real?"

We'd been dating for more than six months when Chris went out of town for work. By his third night away, I was slamming kitchen cabinets, irritable. I was pining for him, but I wasn't about to admit it.

My daughter, on the other hand, asked for his email. Then she left this "sent" message on my laptop: I miss you. I love you.

I sat there and stared at the screen. I'd started to date again when my daughter was a toddler. There was so much at stake, yet I'd initially felt so hopeful about finding love again. I'd imagined meeting the right man when she was still little and blending our families. While that never happened, years later here was my daughter, so open to love.

One year after meeting Chris, we were on a much-treasured dinner date. But Chris was edgy. He downed his cocktail too fast. His shoulders tensed up whenever the waiter came by. As we walked back to his car in silence, he let go of my hand.

"There's something I need to tell you," he said.

I turned around. His eyes were teary.

"I'm sorry, I'm like my mom. I can't talk when I'm emotional."

I thought someone had died.

After pulling a ring from his pocket, Chris tugged out a glittering necklace—for my daughter. He asked if he could join our little family.

"Yes," I whispered.

"Are you sure?" he said.

I was finally ready to open this door. After all, he and my daughter were already there, waiting for me.

Personals

Muriel Johnson

BFWK

Me: single black female with kids, early thirties. Short, overweight, with lots of stretch marks. Looking for handsome male with great body, lots of money, able to accommodate all the desires and needs of a single woman and three children. Must enjoy nature, traveling, reading, dancing, and the arts, and be willing to pay all the time. Needs to be emotionally and financially secure, spiritually grounded, and a philanthropist-type. Must do laundry, dishes, general housecleaning, cooking, and assist with homework.

Must have a valid driver's license, an insured vehicle, preferably a minivan to taxi children to their various extracurricular activities. Must also be skilled in full-body massage and female pampering. Non-smoker, no heavy drinking, no codependencies. Must expect nothing and give unconditionally. Can't wait to meet you!

Kaboom

Susan Goldberg

Here's how it works:

    I see her, standing in the middle of a cobblestoned street in Montreal, holding a small, wet, resigned cat in her two hands. Or she's turned three-quarters of the way toward me at a conference cocktail party, smiling into the middle distance, a heavily tattooed arm raising a drink to her lips. Maybe she's seated on the lip of the low stage at the edge of a throbbing dance floor, beckoning to me through the haze of bodies with her upturned chin as if to say, *Why aren't you already talking to me?* She's the girl with the empty seat next to her at the memoir-writing workshop, the one who escaped her childhood cult, whose sentences I finish and who finishes mine.

    Here's how it works: I see her, and—*kaboom!*—suddenly everyone else in the room; on the cobblestoned street; on the dance floor; at the party, workshop, fades away into the background, fuzzy outlines that throw her into even sharper relief. I move toward her, and I am rendered uncharacteristically and involuntarily bold, intimate.

I introduce myself. I get her a drink (or, if she scans more toward butch, ask her to get me one), trace my finger along the outline of her tattoo as I admire it, hold her hand longer than necessary when we're introduced, touch her shoulder for a long moment as we chat. I lose filters, say things I would normally never be brave enough to say, even fueled by alcohol: *A bunch of us are getting drinks—do you want to join? Here's my number. I'm getting really claustrophobic with all these people around—do you want to go for a walk? I can't quite shake the thought of what it might be like to kiss you.*

I don't pretend I come across as cool and suave as I blurt ridiculous things; I flirt shamelessly, yes, but also awkwardly. Suave isn't really the point. The point is that she is here, and I am here, and in the space between us—a space that I am suddenly and unwaveringly compelled to close—crackles an unmistakable and unbidden force, one far stronger than my usual introvert's urge to quit this party or dance floor or workshop for the uncomplicated quiet of my own room and routine. Not always, but often, it's a force strong enough to bypass obstacles like awkwardness (or, say, heterosexuality, or her marriage)—and she and I find ourselves making out like desperate teenagers in some darkened hallway near the dance floor. Maybe we're together for fifteen minutes, or a night, or on and off again for years. Maybe we move in, get married, have a couple of kids.

That's how it works.

Until it doesn't.

Here, on the other hand, is how it has never worked:

I click on someone's profile and she seems nice enough—decent-looking, kind, smart, intriguing, even. Maybe she wants to build a tiny house one day or is really into fermenting things. Maybe she likes the same authors as me. She's not wearing a baseball cap in her profile picture, knows the difference between *their* and *they're*, doesn't want (more) kids, doesn't wax poetic for paragraphs about her dog, doesn't end every sentence with "lol, you know?" And I click, and she clicks, and we text and chat for a while, and we eventually meet up, and we have a perfectly lovely meal or coffee or drink or walk. And even though there is no sudden thunderclap, no *kaboom* moment of pure and intense focus, I know that she is a good person and a great catch and so I go for it, aware that the longing will come eventually, that I will slowly and steadily fall deeply in love and lust and live happily ever after.

Look. It's not necessarily how I would have made me, either.

Many days, it feels like a design flaw, this insistence on chemistry. Is it cynical that I attribute these *kaboom* moments to chemistry and not romance? Or maybe chemistry and romance are versions of each other, to*may*to to*mah*to: either way, maybe the design flaw isn't so much my insistence on chemistry as it is the relative rarity of the chemistry itself. I've encountered *kaboom* moments maybe ten times in my life (and their absence enough times to serve as a control group), which is sufficient to convince me that the phenomenon is both very, very real and maddeningly elusive. In any case, as much as I might wish for them to happen even just a teensy bit more often than they do, I can't honestly say that I would be willing to dilute their power. I'm no chemist, but I am relatively sure that their potency is inversely related to their scarcity.

This elusiveness, though, is a bit more glaring now that my marriage has ended, especially given that I currently live in a small city where the queer dating pickings are slim. Where I live, Tinder's little homing device *bloop-bloop-bloops* sadly in its concentric circles before letting me know that there's no one new around me and that I should consider changing my settings. OkCupid takes a similar stance when my search for women aged thirty-six to fifty-five within fifty miles turns up precisely zero suitors: "Try broadening your search settings," the app tells me, as though I'm rigid, unadventurous, for refusing to consider the twenty-four-year-old goth who lives in her mom's basement and is really into gaming. Maybe it's my fault that I live in a queer dating desert, these platforms tell me, and if I were more open to dating someone nice in, say, Portland, then I'd have better luck.

And, you know? I would be open to dating someone nice in Portland, which is, really, only three flights and an international border away, if, when I saw her for the first time, before I even knew her name, the rest of the world faded away into the background. But online dating by its very nature doesn't allow for pheromones. Particularly from a distance, online dating requires weeks or months of witty repartee, which maybe turns into phone calls, until you finally meet and there it is—ka-*bust*—precisely no chemistry at all, despite (or maybe because of?) all that time invested.

"I'm done with online dating," I told my friend Jody.

"Is this where I'm supposed to tell you that you're going to find someone now that you've stopped looking?" she asked.

I envisioned myself, disingenuous in the middle of an empty field, yelling, "I'm nooooot loooooooking!" at the sky.

"I'm forty-six," I said, as she nodded. "It's just that my time is too valuable to squander. And I'm kind of grooving on this 'single' thing."

Except when my ex asks me, in September, what my plans are for the holidays so that she can start to book flights for the kids and I think, *Ugh, the holidays*. When my eleven-year-old son compares me to the TV character Jane the Virgin: "Like, you're a single mom. Except, um, that I guess I don't think you're a virgin." When I go solo to weddings, bat mitzvahs.

Except in those moments where I wonder whether a life—my life—contains only a finite number of *kaboom* moments, and whether I have used mine up, all those rare, jaw-dropping, thigh-tensioning thuds of desire, longing, joy.

Except when I wonder whether my insistence on chemistry is less a mark of self-acceptance and adulthood than it is a sign of immaturity, some adolescent dedication to a story I've told myself about who I am and how I love. Maybe I *could* change my settings, tell a different story, open myself to the possibility of a relationship modelled on a slow, controlled burn rather than a Molotov-cocktail ignition. And maybe that story would have a happy ending.

Even if it never has before, counters a little voice inside my head.

Maybe because you never let it.

Maybe because I never had to.

Maybe you should rethink that.

Maybe you should go fu—

And around and around I go, until I get distracted by the next step in my generally full and joyous life. It's by no means perfect, this life, but its imperfect parts wouldn't be solved by the addition of a partner. It's also true that not every *kaboom* girl has been relationship material; some, I'm fairly certain, were *kaboom* girls precisely because they were *not* relationship material. But somewhere in there must be a sweet spot, no? The already charmed life, made that much more complete by an irresistible *and* compatible someone exploding across its path, the fire burning hot and bright and long before fading into embers that we can—and do—tend carefully, bank and stoke and feed, so that the flames keep rising. It's happened before. It may happen again.

And if and when I see her, I'll cross the room and introduce myself.

Because that's how I work.

The loves of my life are my children and my mother. I don't feel as if I need a man.

—Diane Keaton

I Don't Want Your Husband

P. Charlotte Lindsay

Dear Mean Mommies,

I do not want your husbands.

Just because my marriage ended and I find myself a single mom doesn't mean I now covet your man. When I was ten years old, I didn't lie on my canopy bed for hours on end, gazing at my Shaun Cassidy posters, listening to Barry Manilow records, thinking *When I grow up, I want to be a forty-five-year-old woman with two kids, two dogs, two birds, two fish, a mortgage, and no husband.* It's just how life turned out.

That doesn't mean I want your husbands.

Remember when you and the other Mean Mommies stopped including me in your coupled events . . . when I became uncoupled?

I didn't want your husbands then.

Remember that night when "the party was cancelled," so my children and I brought over the chocolate chip cookies we'd baked, just to be nice, and it turns out the party *wasn't* cancelled? There you all were, coupled, with your glasses of champagne and your mouths agape. Remember the uncomfortable silence?

I didn't want your husbands then, either. I did want to climb into my bed and cry. But I didn't, because I have kids.

Mean Mommy Number Three, remember when I asked you, "Why am I not invited anymore?" You shrugged compassionately, "I don't know." I said, "Is it because I'm single?" And you reluctantly answered, "Yes."

Well, I didn't want your husband. I wanted to be Katharine Hepburn, dramatically slap you, throw my scotch in your face, and saunter from the room wearing a fabulous pantsuit. But I didn't. I went home, had a glass of chardonnay with another single mom, and had some laughs. She doesn't want your husbands, either.

I've listened to you complain about your husbands: "He works too much." "He doesn't help around the house." Your sprinkler has been broken for a month. Your trip to Thailand was downgraded to a trip to Hawaii. He got the scent wrong when he bought you that $100 candle. Doesn't he know your favorite candle scent by now? He asked me what scent you like. I guessed. I got it wrong. And I also didn't want him.

The thought of kissing your husband makes me ill. The thought of sleeping with him produces a little bit of vomit in my mouth. You tell me he snores, farts, burps, has erectile dysfunction, and watches too much football. This does not turn me on.

Even if it did, I wouldn't want him.

I don't want your two kids on the weekends. I don't want to deal with his dry cleaning, laundry, and office dramas. I don't want to take care of yet another human being . . . *three* more human beings. And, frankly, I just don't want him!

Ladies, I like your husbands. They are nice. I enjoy conversing with them. They have interesting careers. They ask me about my job. They read books, tell jokes, and some even follow *The Young and the*

Restless. They don't complain about their wives. They gossip a little, but not much. They barbecue.

And they don't want *me* either.

For the record, I would *never* want a friend's husband. Because I am a friend . . . who happens to be single. "Single" is just a tiny a part of me. It does not define me. *You* are defining me. Because you are afraid I will steal your husbands.

Truth be told, deep down you are terrified of me, *not* because I will steal your husbands, but because of what I represent. I am the embodiment of your greatest fear: That your husbands will leave *you*—by divorce, by death, by some unforeseen, unimagined circumstance. You are terrified that you might have to deal with the challenges that come with solo parenting, the stigma you've attached to it. You fear that one day *you* could be the uninvited. You are terrified that your friends will do to you what you've done to others. And that you, too, won't want other women's husbands.

Single parenting is not contagious. It's generally just the byproduct of an ending. Fifty percent of all marriages end—and only a small few result from a woman wanting someone else's husband. Generally, it's just how life turns out.

So now that we've cleared this up, I hope you will include me—invite me to your next soiree, school event, or weekend getaway with the gang. I probably won't go. Because not only do I not want your husbands, I also don't want you. Because you think I want your husbands.

Oh, and by the way, Mrs. Clooney, Mrs. Reynolds, and Mrs. Hemsworth . . .

I want your husbands.

Love,
P. Charlotte Lindsay

How to Love

January Gill O'Neil

After stepping into the world again,
there is that question of how to love,
how to bundle yourself against the frosted morning—
the crunch of icy grass underfoot, the scrape
of cold wipers along the windshield—
and convert time into distance.

What song to sing down an empty road
as you begin your morning commute?
And is there enough in you to see, really see,
the three wild turkeys crossing the street
with their featherless heads and stilt-like legs
in search of a morning meal? Nothing to do
but hunker down, wait for them to safely cross.

As they amble away, you wonder if they want
to be startled back into this world. Maybe you do, too,

waiting for all this to give way to love itself,
to look into the eyes of another and feel something—
the pleasure of a new lover in the unbroken night,
your wings folded around him, on the other side
of this ragged January, as if a long sleep has ended.

You Can't "Undo" This One

Jessica Bern

As I entered the restaurant, I saw the lights dim. To the couples in the room, the message was clear: "Romance time!" To me, it was more like, "Please leave, you're killing our vibe." I'd dined in this place many times—it was my kitchen away from my kitchen, you could say. It was also my refuge; a place where the staff made me feel like I was always welcome.

Until that night, it had been two years since I'd gone beyond a phone call with a guy. I was a forty-two-year-old single mother, underemployed, and living with my toddler in Los Angeles.

I had been through too many horrible dates and mini-relationships, and I was tired. There had been the real estate agent who was only interested in me because he wanted the listing for my house. There was the guy who thought he was moving in with me after two dates because no woman had ever tolerated him for that long. And, of course, there was the angry actor who asked me for eight hundred dollars to cover his parking tickets. The worst was the guy I spoke to for hours over the course of several weeks, his voice often the last one I heard before my head hit the pillow. I was on my own for the first time in fourteen years and felt so low. I shared my life and my secrets with him, only to find out his pictures were fake, as was every single thing he told me about himself.

Then there was the night when I followed a friend's suggestion to get dressed up and wander through a bookstore because, "You love to read, and if you meet a guy there, chances are he loves to read, too, and what the hell, what have you got to lose?" Well, as it turns out, my dignity, as well as any hope of ever meeting anyone at a bookstore.

After all this, I had put up many barriers. That this man had gotten through all of them spoke volumes. I had been talking and texting with Paul all week. His profile photos showed a man in his mid-forties with kind eyes and a great smile. Everything about him read "easygoing," a quality I really wanted in a partner. He was also kind and funny, and I was so looking forward to meeting him.

One of the waitresses, Kelly, stopped by my table. A junior at the local community college, she had pale skin, blue eyes, and a tattoo of a zipper on the back of her neck. Every time I saw it, I imagined pulling it down just so I could see what was inside. Out of habit, Kelly assumed I was alone and started to take away the other place setting. "I'm actually meeting someone," I told her. "He just texted to say he'll be here in a minute." Kelly's eyes widened. Since we met, I'd had the feeling that I was a constant reminder of how her life could be so much worse. Now, apparently, the thought that she'd have to suddenly find a replacement was making it difficult for her to respond.

Paul walked in. He looked just like his photos, and from the expression on his face, it appeared he was pleased to see me as well. Oh, miracle! As soon as he sat down, the conversation started to flow. As we talked about being single parents, our kids, and the places we wanted to visit when they were grown, the potential for something long-term didn't seem as absurd as it had in the past. I was actually getting a little excited. I couldn't help but think, Could this be it? No more dying alone? Maybe we could go see Hearst Castle, and we could have dinner parties and game nights and everything else I missed so much from when I was married. I was unbelievably thirsty for love and companionship, and here was the proverbial tall human glass of water.

Kelly returned and took our orders. She appeared to have recovered from the shock and awe of me possibly having a life. Right after she left, Paul got up and went to the men's room. As soon as he disappeared, my heart sank. I had been through so many "This is it!" moments that as soon as he was out of sight, I started wondering if this was just another false alarm.

I took my phone out of my purse. I ignored the instinct to put on my glasses and texted my sister: "I feel like all I will ever be with in my life are losers." About a nanosecond, after I hit "send," I glanced back at the screen and through the blurry haze, I noticed that I hadn't sent the text to my sister. I had sent it to Paul, my date.

Panicking, my eyes darting back and forth. I looked for something, someone, to undo what I had just done. Undo, undo, undo! I was yelling inside my head. I spent hours every day on my computer, and I could practically feel my fingers searching for the buttons on my keyboard.

Paul returned to the table. "Did you read my text?" I asked, half laughing, half trying not to cry. "Nope," he replied. Relieved, I told him what it said and then tried to explain that I didn't mean *he* was the loser—that, in fact, I really liked him. Even though he seemed almost entertained by what just happened, I could sense I'd lost him. His eyes went flat, and any sexual energy between us melted away. I was no longer someone with potential; I was just some cute loon recounting a wacky story that he found amusing, almost as if it involved me and another guy altogether.

We went for ice cream afterward, sat on a bench outside the shop, and talked for another hour. He then walked me to my car

258 | We Got This

and even kissed me goodnight. After not hearing from him for a few days, I texted to thank him for a great evening. He never responded.

Embarrassed, I did what I always do, which was to make light of the situation, play it for laughs. That's how I often deal with the pain of life. It wasn't until months later that I realized that my need to not be alone was greater than my attraction to Paul.

I no longer regret what happened on that date. It taught me valuable life lessons: You must be happy on your own before you can be OK in the company of others—and always put on your glasses before you text someone.

I Ask the Impossible

Ana Castillo

I ask the impossible: love me forever.
Love me when all desire is gone.
Love me with the single-mindedness of a monk.
When the world in its entirety,
and all that you hold sacred, advise you
against it: love me still more.
When rage fills you and has no name: love me.
When each step from your door to your job tires you—
love me; and from job to home again.

Love me when you're bored—
When every woman you see is more beautiful than the last,
or more pathetic, love me as you always have:
not as admirer or judge, but with
the compassion you save for yourself
in your solitude.

Love me as you relish your loneliness,
the anticipation of your death,
mysteries of the flesh, as it tears and mends.
Love me as your most treasured childhood memory—
and if there is none to recall—
imagine one, place me there with you.
Love me withered as you loved me new.

Love me as if *I* were forever—
and I will make the impossible
a simple act,
by loving you, loving you as I do.

Chapter Seven:
Here Comes the Sun

Still I Rise

—Maya Angelou

Yeah, But . . .

Cheryl Dumesnil

I'm back in my old neighborhood, where my ex still lives, at the annual Fourth of July block party. My two kids have disappeared somewhere in the mix of doughnuts and water balloon fights. My ex is weaving through the crowd, holding her cell phone aloft, showing her long-distance girlfriend, via FaceTime, what the Fourth looks like around here. I'm standing in the dappled shade of a live oak, introducing my fiancée, Sarah, to the people I lived near and raised my kids with for 10 years. They're as close to family as nonfamily gets, these neighbors, and it feels just so right to integrate my old and new worlds this way.

As Sarah is called away to watch my youngest son perform a "sick trick" on the blow-up water slide, my friend David says, "She seems lovely."

Three kids barrel toward us on Razor scooters. We step out of their path. The closed street is a mess of streamer-laced bikes, discarded coffee cups, tables laden with potluck food, and lawn chairs gathered in circles.

"She really is," I agree. "It may seem like she's being nice just so you'll like her, but she's actually that nice."

"I'm so glad you found someone," David says, the sincerity apparent in his eyes.

"What I love most about this whole thing," I say, "is that it came as such a surprise. After the divorce, I was ready to spend the rest of my life on my own."

"Oh, come on," David says. "Really?"

"Really," I nod.

How do I explain this? My marriage broke, irreparably, years before it ended. I had done my level best to create a healthy life for myself and my kids, despite the brokenness, hoping someday, eventually, maybe my ex and I could fix it. This was a lot like trying to live a fulfilling life while a shark is eating your leg. You're telling yourself, *Hey, look at all I have to be grateful for! Look how wonderful my children are! I have such lovely friends! Look at the amazing work I get to do!* And your friends are like, *Uh, do you not know a shark is eating your leg?* And you're all, *Shark? Meh. It's not that bad. I'm used to it.* Until the shark swims away, and you're like, *Whoa! Why the fuck did I live like that for so long?*

For some people, divorce kicks off a journey of self-discovery. For others, it kicks off a no-holds-barred tour of Tinder. Me? I found joy in my individuality. Turns out that the peace I had sought for years—in therapy, yoga, books, solo retreats, and self-help conferences—came to me much more easily *without a fucking shark gnawing on my leg.*

Of course, it hurt to give up my long-held hope for a healthy marriage. Of course, it hurt—and it still hurts—to split my children's belongings and time between two houses. Of course, it hurt to see how the divorce disrupted their lives. And it hurt to leave my old neighborhood, where heartfelt interactions occurred daily among friends, not because we'd planned them, but simply because two people happened to walk out to their mailboxes at the same time. I miss that.

But after years of trying to shore up a fractured marriage, I found a certain empowerment in calling things what they were. While I was married, I'd felt, in so many ways, like a solo mom, handling the vast majority of the childrearing on my own. Now I could rightfully claim the title that fit my experience. I'd felt lonely in my marriage, but now that I was actually alone, the feeling of loneliness dissolved.

And something else happened. The night my ex told me she was moving out, I said—as much to myself as to her, "If you go, I will grow to a size that no longer fits in this marriage." She went. I grew. And God, I *loved* the growing.

I tell David, "After the divorce, the only relationship I was interested in was between myself and the larger mysteries of the Universe."

David raises his eyebrows and nods, as if this is an idea he's never considered.

"A couple friends tried to fix me up with people, but I was like, 'Nope. No interest. If someone comes along and blindsides me, I'll pay attention, but I'm definitely not looking.'"

I don't even trust the idea of "looking." In my experience, the looking changes what I see. As soon as I ask, "Could she be the one?" the internal compromising begins. So, no looking for me. Just living. On my own. Happily.

Though at times I felt utterly overwhelmed by the trifecta of responsibilities—raising kids, making money, and keeping house— that was no reason to couple up. At forty-five years old, I had some questions about how I'd support myself, how I'd handle retirement, illnesses, or aging on my own. But when those questions floated to the surface, so did an abiding faith that I'd find a way. Meanwhile, I was content on my own, guiding my life by my intuition, watching my path unfold one true step into the next. In fact, I loved it.

"Well," David says, coming in for a hug. "It's so good to see you so happy."

Something within me flinches. What is it, that tic? "Thanks,"

I say, brushing it off, wrapping my arms around my friend. "It really is the sweetest surprise."

Blindsided is not the right metaphor for the way Sarah entered my life. It had more grace than that, like the annual arrival of monarch butterflies in the eucalyptus grove near Natural Bridges Beach. First one flutters in, then the next, then dozens more, until their wings fill the trees, an otherworldly presence painting the branches orange.

"I keep getting this feeling someone is coming into my life," I once wrote in my journal. "Someone from the past I'm going to meet again. I'm not feeling a need to do anything about this, to take any action. It's just a curiosity. Things will unfold on their own."

Never did I think that "someone" could be Sarah. Not even after I dreamt that friends had taken me to a coffee shop to show me Sarah working behind the bar. "She's back," one friend told me. "She's been here for months," the other said.

That's how I'd met Sarah in real life, at a coffee shop, ten years ago. She was the twenty-something barista behind the counter; I was the thirty-something married customer, with a toddler in tow and super pregnant belly. The first time I spoke to Sarah, she felt instantly famil-iar—as if she and I had been best buddies at sleepaway camp, then found each other again decades later. Her sea-glass blue eyes looked surprised when she saw me approaching the counter. Not, "Hi, what can I get for you today?" but "Oh, it's you!" As for my eyes? I imagine she could see the curiosity behind them, the unspoken "Have I met you before?"

It didn't take long for Sarah to became my go-to friend, a part of my family. My oldest son, then two years old, called her "My Sarah." My infant son slept as easily in her arms as he did in his moms'. At a time when I desperately needed someone to hold a mirror up and reflect my best self to me, Sarah did. At a time when Sarah, who was just starting to come out to her friends and family, needed to see what her future could look like—wife and wife, raising kids, living openly in their community—my family showed her that. What I didn't show her were the ever-widening fissures in my marriage. As I turned my attention to patching them up, Sarah and I lost touch.

My marriage repair mission failed, clearly. Eight years later, as my ex and I were finalizing the details of our divorce, an email sailed in from across the country, from Sarah.

First one monarch . . .

I read it while standing on the sidewalk outside a restaurant in San Francisco, waiting for friends. "Sarah! No way!" I responded. "You were in my dream a couple nights ago . . . "

Then another . . .

Over the following months, bit by bit, we filled each other in on all we had missed: the teardown and rebuilding of my life, my "babies" who were now nine and eleven years old, her cross-country move and quiet mountain lifestyle, her looming questions about the relationship she was in, her unfathomable adoration of her two-year-old niece.

Then another . . .

"Would you ever get married again?" she asked me once, a hypothetical question.

"I'm happy on my own," I told her. "I'm not opposed to marriage in theory, but I'm not looking for it either. It would have to be like icing on top of my already awesome life cake."

Sarah listened and supported me through the final stages of my divorce negotiations. I listened and supported her as she came to terms with the end of her relationship.

Then another . . .

In my journal, I wrote, "She's always understood me, no explanation necessary. God, it feels good to be known."

Then dozens more, until . . .

Two years later, Sarah and I are at Natural Bridges Beach with my kids. We're watching them hunt for treasures we've hidden in the sand. They dig out seashells inked with the words, "Coming soon... to a City Hall Near You... on September 21... We're getting married!"

... an otherworldly presence, the whole grove glowing.

A friend from my old neighborhood, Shelly, has dropped by for a glass of wine and a chat while our kids hang out together in the back room. She's looking at wedding photos we recently hung on the living room wall—Sarah and me sitting on the front bumper of a light blue VW bus, leaning into each other, holding hands. Sarah's wearing a strapless, baby blue dress she found on eBay and a cream-colored, beaded cardigan I bought at a thrift shop two decades ago. I'm wearing a forest green dress I found in my closet and a vintage cardigan, baby blue, rescued from a second-hand shop years ago.

We got married exactly the way we wanted to—a tiny ceremony at San Francisco City Hall, a trip to our favorite ice cream shop afterward, a tour of the city in that VW bus with the kids and my parents along for the ride, tattoos instead of wedding rings. When people ask me about the day, I say, "Everyone should have that much fun getting married."

In the photo Shelly's looking at, the only thing brighter than our *I-can't-believe-we-get-to-do-this* smiles is the sunlight gleaming off the top of the bus, haloing the crowns of our heads.

That's how every day feels: *I can't believe we get to do this.*

"I'm so glad you're happy," Shelly says.

I take the sentiment as I know she means it: *Girl, I watched you walk barefoot across the hot coals of divorce, and now here you are.* "Thanks, Shel," I say.

But again, that flinch inside. The same one I felt when David and so many others have said some version of "It's so good to see you happy." What *is* that?

Of course, I *am* happy. Beyond happy. The love I experience with Sarah has transformed my understanding of love; it has expanded my capacity for joy; it has connected me more deeply to the very mysteries of the Universe I'd planned to relate to *by myself* for the rest of my life. This sounds like hyperbole, but actually it's a carefully calibrated statement of fact.

Yes, I'm *that* happy.

So, what's the glitch? Why, when people comment on my happiness, do I want to say, "Yeah, but . . ." Yeah, but . . . *what*?

This morning, the question lingered. After dropping my kids off at school, instead of heading home to work, I followed my instinct to the Lafayette Reservoir. I needed to think, so I needed to hike.

On this breezeless day, the reservoir mirrored everything around it—the trees that ring the bank, the autumn-blue sky, the feathery white clouds, an osprey circling overhead. As I climbed the first hill of the loop trail, I brought the question back to my mind: Yeah, but . . . what? Among the fallen oak leaves and birdsong, the answer came: Yeah, but . . . *I was already happy before Sarah.*

To the friends who witnessed it, my life reads like a semi-traditional fairytale that culminates in a happily-ever-after wedding. But there's an important difference. Fairytales begin with a damsel in distress and, let's be honest, they end in a textbook codependent relationship likely to deteriorate as the damsel realizes her own power or as the savior gets sick of saving, whichever comes first.

My love story goes like this: The thing I'd refused to let happen for years—a divorce—finally happened. I embraced that change of circumstances and, on my own, I built my happiness, brick by brick, with my own blistered hands. I found peace, strength, and fulfillment on my own, and I felt proud of that. I was good with that. And then . . .

My Birth, My Way

Cate Morrissey

I felt like I had fallen into a bad dream.

I was pregnant, and I was leaving my husband—two life occurrences that, theoretically, should never mix. Just as the morning sickness abated, just as the baby began to make movements that I could feel, my ex-husband committed an act of physical abuse, and I made the choice to leave.

When I visited a divorce attorney, my belly was round, and my bladder was pressed by the weight of the baby. For the rest of my pregnancy, I waddled in and out of that office, a new solo mom in shock. The staff asked how I was feeling, how the baby was doing. My lawyer asked repeatedly whether I was ready to file for divorce yet.

"Not until after the baby comes," I said. "I don't want to do this now."

I wanted to give him time to show up—like, *really* show up. To apologize. To go to therapy. To make an effort to be a better man, a better husband, a better father. To save our marriage. But he didn't.

My nurse midwife spent extra time with me during my prenatal appointments. Emotionally, I had become high risk. She was no doubt screening me for signs of depression related to my impending divorce. She also must have been concerned that I might return to my husband—a man who had proven through multiple incidents that he was not safe.

We spoke at length about the birth. My midwife understood my wishes for an unmedicated water birth if at all possible. She knew I wanted to labor at home for as long as I could. But when we began to discuss who would be there—in the room, during the birth—it felt like all the air got sucked out of me.

My ex wanted to be there. He was insisting. It was his right, he said, to be present when our child was born. Legally, I knew he was wrong. There was nothing in the law that prevented me from keeping him away. But I felt guilty anyway. Just a few months prior, we had been preparing for this baby together.

In the back of my mind, I wondered, would being present provide the epiphany he needed to finally get help? Would it be the reconnection that would save our marriage?

My midwife asked me more specifically, "Do you want *him* there? Would you feel safe?"

I didn't know.

During one of my prenatal appointments, my doula looked me in the eyes and said, "This isn't about him. I want you to take all of the energy you're focusing on him and refocus it on yourself and that baby."

And she was right.

My pregnancy had been largely overshadowed by the stress of the divorce, and by continued physical and emotional abuse perpetrated by my ex. Life felt like a carnival of hormones and emotions. I was angry and sad. My stress was through the roof. I felt betrayed and railroaded. I was relieved to be away from him, but I also still loved him. I was terribly confused. I could barely focus on the new life I was growing inside my body.

One sleepless night, the emotional dam broke. I flipped on the bedside light, grabbed a notebook, and wrote my "birth manifesto." My feelings, needs, and desires came tumbling out onto paper. The words were fierce and honest and unapologetic, raw and angry and hurt.

Finally, I thought, Mama Bear is showing up.

In my journal, I claimed the right to feel safe, the right to labor and deliver on my own terms. I claimed the right to focus all my energy on myself and the baby, the right to control who was present. And I claimed my right to *not* feel guilty about it.

I did not want to be watched or judged by my ex. I did not want him to take the baby from my arms right away. I wanted space and calm and peace. During the birth, I wanted support from women I trusted.

"Women do not need men to do the tremendous work of birth," I wrote, and then underlined. "We are warrioresses, and we can do it by our own damn selves."

The birth was long and hard. I moaned and screamed my way to the finish line, until finally the baby slipped into the arms of the midwife. His wet little body was placed on my chest, where he was rubbed until his purplish hue became pink and he began to cry. I was surrounded by women. Women who honored me. Women who helped me to bed and brushed the hair from my eyes and told me how well I had done.

And when I looked at my son, I did not regret for one second my decision to birth on my own.

"This is what a mother is," I remember whispering to him. "I will always protect you."

How I Came to Me

Malaika King Albrecht

No longer am I
dispossessed
or repossessed.

I am possessed.
I am in possession
of myself.

I am self-possessed.
The sun rises in my throat
and burns a perfect hole

in my forehead
where cliff swallows roost.
Each raindrop falls

perfectly into place
on the greenness of me.
I want you to know

that at this edge
of my life:
I will jump.

I will jump.
I will jump
and I will fly.

I'm prouder of my years as a single mother than any other part of my life.

—J. K. Rowling

Teacher and Teammate

Sarah Kowalski

"Mama, don't worry, I can transform into anything you need with my special powers," my son Aiden exclaimed, while I grumbled about not being able to find a spatula to flip his pancake. His batman cape fluttered as he jumped off a chair, landing with a modest thud. He quickly righted his ever-present firefighter helmet and brightly added, "Did you know that, Mama? I can be whatever you need."

Yes, I know that.

Three-year-old Aiden is obsessed with firefighters, superheroes, and construction workers. He's constantly staging rescues, checking a room for danger before he lets me enter, and transforming into what I need. It melts my heart, making both my painful path to becoming a mother and the struggle of raising a son alone less and less consequential with each passing day.

Motherhood didn't turn out the way I planned. In fact, it dashed every expectation of what I thought my journey to becoming a mom would look like. But that journey also prepared me for the day-to-day rigors of parenting alone.

Unlike many solo moms, I entered motherhood knowing full well I would be raising my child alone. It wasn't my first choice. I'd always dreamed of having a partner and creating a child who was a blend of the two of us. I imagined gazing at my baby and guessing which traits and characteristics came from me or my husband.

But life didn't happen that way. By the time I was 40, with no partner in sight, I realized if I wanted to have a child, I would need to do it alone, using a sperm donor. However, the disappointment didn't end there. When I finally decided to greenlight project solo mom, I visited my OB/GYN to get the rundown on insemination. As I sat on the crinkly white butcher paper covering the exam table, my doctor stated, a little too casually for my liking, "If you want to get pregnant, you will more than likely need to use an egg donor." I was floored—declared infertile before I even began trying to conceive.

I left the doctor's office incensed. Now my reluctantly revised dream of parenthood would need to be revised again? I would need to give up having a genetic connection to my child? This idea stretched too far beyond my vision of motherhood.

Over the next few days, I mulled over my doctor's advice. Was there any point in pursuing an egg donor? No. I didn't want to conceive a child with whom I had no genetic connection. I would either beat the odds and conceive with my eggs or remain childless.

My quest to beat the odds meant signing on for austere diets, consuming mountains of supplements, and visiting every alternative healer I could find. I cannot begin to count how many hours I spent driving from one practitioner's office to the next, not to mention how much money I forked over. Perhaps even worse was the self-hatred I met along the way—torturous glimpses into my psyche at the shame, anger, and hurt I harbored over my infertility. Worst of all? In the end, it didn't work. It looked like I would remain childless.

Or would I?

One bright autumn day, I followed the sun's invitation to practice qigong on my back deck. As I drenched myself in sunlight and listened to the birds busily chirping, I travelled deep into meditation, feeling vast and filled with light. With that clarity, I decided to reconsider the egg donor question. Was a genetic link to my child essential to what I wanted from motherhood?

Sitting at the table on my back deck, I wrote in my journal: "Do I want to be a mother if it means using an egg donor?"

First, the objection came: "It's not supposed to be this way—having a baby means having a genetic link." Instead of stopping there, as I had in the past, I continued, asking "Why?"

Did I feel a need to pass on my genes or to carry on a legacy? No, neither reason rang true for me.

I could argue that using someone else's eggs would create an information gap—I wouldn't know much about the donor's genetic and medical history. Then again, no one has an impeccable genetic history—my future child could end up with better or worse genes than mine.

I continued from a different angle: "What aspects of being a mother depend on a genetic connection?" I couldn't come up with a single one. I was head over heels in love with both of my rescue dogs, and we weren't even the same species. Heck, if someone handed me any baby to care for, I would have fallen in love instantly—no gene-sharing necessary. Sure, I would have loved to have seen what aspects of myself expressed in my child, but this wasn't necessary to my finding fulfillment as a mother.

Then what was I looking for in motherhood? I was looking for purpose. I was ready to give up the spontaneity and freedom of my adult years to embrace the needs of a child. I wanted to watch someone grow up, to see the world through their eyes, and to selflessly devote my time and energy to raising a fabulous human being. This yearning didn't require a genetic link.

So I could get my head around giving up the genetic connection, but I still wanted to experience pregnancy and to nurse my baby. I decided to use an egg donor.

As hard as the decision was to make, once I made it, I felt tremendous relief. Finally, I could say "when I get pregnant" instead of "if I get pregnant." I would still hit some bumps along the way—as if life wanted to remind me, once again, that nothing ever goes according to plan. But in the end, I lucked out. We lucked out. I got pregnant on the first try.

As I snuggled in bed with Aiden this morning, his head on my chest, my arm locked under his body, he refused to let me get up, insisting we trade I love you's. "I love you, honey," he said. "I love you, sweet pea," I responded. "I love you, pancake," he said in his goofiest voice. We play this game often—coming up with increasingly silly foods, trying to outdo each other. We were late waking up, yet I stayed, breathing in my little guy, my heart about to burst out of my chest, as I responded, "I love you, green bean," as he fell apart giggling.

The love I feel for Aiden is what every mother tries but can't quite seem to describe, though mothering without a partner or family close by hasn't been easy. After three years, I am—thankfully—finally catching up on sleep. Still, everything falls to me—meal planning, decisions big and small, bedtime routines, house upkeep, pet care, financial stability. For the most part, if I find myself in a jam, I have to either work out a solution myself or pay someone to help me. Yes, that is incredibly stressful at times.

Yet there's also a simplicity in mothering solo. I don't endure the stresses I hear my partnered friends talk about—there's no debate about the division of labor; I'm never disappointed by a partner who fails to come home from work on time; I'm never upset by a partner who doesn't step in to give me a day off. I'm never forced to compromise—well, at least not with anyone but my son. I'll never face a custody battle or debate with a partner over what's best for our child. If I want input, I consult a trusted friend, but I can always walk away if I feel unsupported or misunderstood or if I simply disagree with their perspective. See? Simple.

I won't lie: sometimes the lack of kid-free time nearly breaks me—the repetitive games, the tantrums, and the endless boundary testing and potty-training accidents. Ironically, it was my messy path to motherhood that trained me to handle these challenging moments. It taught me to surrender in the face of chaos, to let go of what I cannot control. Some days, I feel like an unstoppable force, able to handle just about anything. Every day, I can't believe I almost gave this up.

The small size of our family means my son and I are an intimately linked duo. We harmonize and evolve together with each passing day. Take the other morning. Getting ready for his first day at preschool, Aiden was melting down because he wanted a different pair of pants. I had checked everywhere but couldn't find the pair he wanted.

After my third trip back upstairs to search, I surrendered. Exasperated, I sat down next to my son at the bottom of the stairs. Internally, I was berating myself for being disorganized, and I was furious at my son for refusing to let it go. That preschooler rigidity was about to push me over the edge.

Then, out of nowhere, an idea came to me. "Are we a team?" I asked, looking into his inky black eyes glistening with fresh tears.

His nose crinkled with displeasure. "Yep, we are Team Mama and Aiden," he mumbled.

I gingerly put my arm around him, sensing he was calming down and would not reflexively shrug off my touch. "Then you need to help Team Mama and Aiden by going to school with the pants you have on."

"But . . . " He began to pull away from me, almost wiggling out from under my touch.

I cut off his whining, "I tried my best, and I cannot find your pants. It would really help our team if you could go to school today in the pants you are already wearing."

Aiden paused, settling into my embrace, looking down at the toy in his hand while he pondered what I'd said. Then he looked up at me with gleaming eyes and exclaimed, "Sure, Mama. We can only do our best. Let's go to school, Team."

Disaster averted, and we actually got to school on time.

The Sky Is Everywhere

Nancy Sharp

It's June 17, 2005, over a year since Brett died, and I still haven't taken the twins to visit his cemetery. The "Daddy is hiding" phase has passed, or at least they no longer verbalize such claims. Jill, a social worker we've seen since the kids were born prematurely, still comes to the apartment, and we're still seeing Dr. Spiegel. Slowly, the intensity of the twins' fears has lessened.

Enough so that while driving to my parents' house in Easton, I decide to casually point out a neighboring cemetery, just to see the sort of reaction it triggers. The kids are sensitive about all things related to illness and death and instantly begin to make connections.

Rebecca holds an imaginary phone to her ear. "Hi, Daddy. I miss you," she sings.

She's in a chatty mood and tells Casey that even though they can't see Daddy anymore they can still talk to him. This is language straight from Jill, and an early indicator of the presupposed role Rebecca assumes as the older twin and, hence, big sister.

Casey, however, offers his own explanation. "We can't see Daddy because he's in the sky." His tone is so calm and certain that I wonder if he's thought about this before.

I grab the steering wheel harder.

Rebecca is confused. "Is the sky back that way, Mama?" she asks, pointing to what she believes is the direction of home.

Now I'm hypervigilant, thinking about how to answer the question.

But I don't ponder long, since Casey, in the same confident tone, does the job. "No, Rebecca, the sky is everywhere."

The sky is everywhere!

What a startling, perfect truth the twins have decoded: *Daddy is in the sky, and the sky is everywhere.*

I'm so happy that I want to pull the car over and hug them close. I commit to remembering this moment forever.

Divorce Cliché

Shannon Lell

In the beginning, after filing and him leaving, on weekend nights without my kids I'd drink red wine and sing sad songs while crying. When it was warm, I took these sad song soirées to my back porch. Inside, the house felt too claustrophobic—the house we'd bought when we got married. I needed to breathe to sing.

Waking up to an empty bottle and a headache, I felt like a failure, though no one was there to judge me except the cats and their cold stares from the nightstand. But one morning, my neighbor of eight years stopped me in the driveway, "I heard you last night—" I didn't let her finish that sentence before I ran away.

Clichés are the death of good writing. I know this. I'm a professional. They're lazy, a sign of immaturity, a lack of creativity on the author's part. But in the months after divorcing, that's what I'd become—one big cliché:

Mid—OK, late—thirties, female, newly divorced with two small kids, seeks red wine for comfort. Lurks on dating websites while singing

Sam Smith's "Stay with Me" at high volume. Dives headlong into yoga. Buys vibrators off Amazon. Contemplates her first tattoo. Starts to empathize with Mrs. Robinson.

See?

I spent months in the shell-shocked aftermath trying to find one safe place to take one clean breath. *If you can just breathe, maybe you'll live.*

Safe places are hard to come by when you feel like the world is watching you, trying to figure out how they'll never *be* you—a wine-soaked divorcée singing John Legend's "All of Me" in the middle of the night on her back porch, a cautionary tale. Hard to come by when a pile of dusty snorkel gear sends you into the blast zone, so you have to sit down on the garage floor to steady yourself. *Breathe, just breathe.*

At some point, I began the cleanup process—cleaned out closets stuffed with mementos and changed the passwords, the locks on the house, the paint in my bedroom—all the while feeling like people were watching me to see what kind of ending I would spin from this sad story. *No one wants to hear about your panic attack over the stack of animal-themed holiday cards you found in the back of your drawer, the ones you had been saving up for him in all those years you'd planned on being together.* The hardest cleanup—the one of my heart—happens alone or with red wine and Brandi Carlile and singing.

And so it continued, the story of the divorce cliché, until one day, two years on, when my daughter asked to see pictures from when she was a baby, and we pulled out the album with her father in it, and it didn't hurt. It didn't feel good; but it didn't hurt. The wine stayed corked in the bottle.

And years later, when my neighbor showed up at my door with tears in her eyes, and I poured her a glass of wine and I listened, I could say, "It's OK. I understand." I could tell her, "There's nothing wrong with taking the path of least resistance for a while, even if it means reducing yourself to a mindless cliché while your neighbors listen." I could promise, "It doesn't feel like it, but one day, you will find your way up to the surface again. You will breathe. But the only way to get there is to sit down, let the pain come, and turn up the sad songs. And then get back up again and keep moving."

Sunday

January Gill O'Neil

You are the start of the week
or the end of it, and according
to The Beatles you creep in
like a nun. You're the second
full day the kids have been
away with their father, the second
full day of an empty house.
Sunday, I've missed you. I've been
sitting in the backyard with a glass
of Pinot waiting for your arrival.
Did you know the first Sweet 100s
are turning red in the garden,
but the lettuce has grown
too bitter to eat. I am looking
up at the bluest sky I have ever seen,
cerulean blue, a heaven sky

no one would believe I was under.
You are my witness. No day
is promised. You are absolution.
You are my unwritten to-do list,
my dishes in the sink, my brownie
breakfast, my braless day.

Why I Don't Grieve for My Daughter at College

Ylonda Gault

I call the oldest of my three children my "first love."

When Chloe was born, my heart didn't merely skip a beat. It found a new syncopation.

Now my "baby" is away at Spelman College, almost nine-hundred miles from my New Jersey home. Her laughter no longer rings through the house. Night after night, I look at her vacant seat at the dinner table. Friends, and even relative strangers, warned me of the devastation.

But it's been almost four months since I last saw Chloe.

And you know what? I'm good. In fact, I'm better than just good.

I don't feel like a part of me is missing. On a primal level, part of all my kids are inside me. All the time. My best friend is not gone; my daughter is. The one I was supposed to train up in the way she should *go*; "go" is the operative word here.

My eyes have shed no tears. I am not depressed, not even a little bit melancholy. No spasms of deep longing when I pass her empty bed, neatly made since she left for college in August. Finally, I understand the grating, coffee mug proverb of modern black women everywhere: "Girl, I am too blessed to be stressed!"

Chloe—the beat of my heart—is stepping into her destiny. And I could not be more proud. Her younger sister and brother—who, admittedly, leave me little time to mourn—have a shining example of achievement.

Of course, thanks to her generation's texting proclivities, I am— in some ways—closer to Chloe than ever. She went vintage shopping recently, for example, and sent me dressing room pictures of each of the secondhand contenders. Things were sometimes rocky between us when she was in high school, and she didn't usually want my advice. Now I was flattered to be invited to weigh in, and I duly praised each outfit.

Chloe's dad and I divorced when she was in high school, leaving her a lot of emotional obstacles to overcome. (It's cool; my kids are all used to my writing about them.) She took her snarky sense of humor and age-appropriate eye-rolls to new heights. But in her absence, I find myself lauding her for the things she did around the house, including her Martha Stewart–level laundry skills and smack-your-mama mac- and-cheese dishes.

I would have liked to have her home to make one of those at Thanksgiving, but she wasn't here. She spent it with my sister and brother in Western New York, in part because she'll be coming home for winter break tomorrow.

Just as her siblings and I have adjusted to our household without her, she has grown used to her freedom, so I imagine there may be some issues in the weeks that she's home. We will probably all fall back into our old roles, slightly reshaped. And then in January she will leave again, and we will adjust once more.

To me, the college send-off was not a blues for Chloe. It was a celebration. And no one was partying harder than our ancestors, who missed out on the luxury of rolling up into hallowed institutions with pining parents in their wake.

I never took college for granted. My mama grew up in the Jim Crow South and never gave serious thought to higher education. My dad didn't even finish high school. So when I stepped across the stage at Northwestern University, glad-handing the robe-wearing strangers who placed the embossed leather folder in my hand, I was entering a world my family had never known. It meant honor. It meant prestige. And it spelled victory.

Privilege takes many forms. I can only assume that the legions of parents who spent this fall up in their feelings over their babies' departures have led lives very different from my own.

But a part of me simply wonders, "Isn't this what we as parents *want* to happen?" There is a natural order to it all. Right? Now I can't lie. There are moments when I worry about Chloe. But I worried a bit when she started full-day preschool, went to sleepaway camp, and, perhaps most terrifying, drove to the mall for the first time. As I did in those times, I talk myself down with faith that angels are with her when I can't be. In other words—grace.

But unlike in the early days of parenting, I now have lots of reasons to have faith in Chloe herself.

She is a competent young woman. She makes sound decisions, chooses decent friendships, and navigates the world with an inner knowingness that has always belied her age.

This is no humblebrag. Much of who she is, quite honestly, has little to do with me. Chloe came into the world with a live-out-loud, kick-ass boldness and an innate ability to self-regulate to a certain extent. She inherited the spiritual DNA of her grandmother and the strong black women who preceded her.

That's why I could've almost scripted the parting scene when I dropped her off at college. After several days spent unpacking, shopping, and shopping some more—it was that time. We said our "goodbye" in the middle of campus after a beautiful rah-rah program to close out orientation. We hugged tightly, kissed—then looked around the yard.

Snot-nosed grown women were everywhere—practically collapsing in sorrow. Chloe said something like, "These moms are, like, legit-shook." We giggled a bit.

Then, "See you, Mom."

Deconstructing Kanji

Mika Yamamoto

The Japanese woman wears a lavender kimono and sits on her knees by the *irori*—the sunken hearth—stabbing at the fire, using the force of *kuyashimi*. The English language fails the Japanese woman who sacrifices her life to her cheating husband, for no single English word expresses her experience. No word captures how the Japanese woman feels as she continues with her duties, tends to the household, stays silent, and maintains an impeccable bun. She does not take herself to bed, wail, or throw dishes. No. She is polite to her cheating husband. She disrupts nobody's life. She bears all the grief alone. She does not share her struggles with anyone; the irori is her only witness. Kuyashimi evokes the physical resistance required of the body to hold this all in; no English word has such power.

This Japanese woman is not me, nor is she anyone I know. It is true that when I was sixteen, my friend shared with me a story about how he had witnessed his mother's kuyashimi. In 1988, though, his mother was not wearing a kimono and tending the irori. The Japanese Woman is purely fiction: a powerful fiction.

294 | We Got This

The Japanese Woman was a dominant image of who I was not—who I never could or would be. Born and raised in Skokie, Illinois, I grew up an Oriental Girl, or maybe a Japanese Girl. Then, when I was fifteen, I moved to Japan and stopped being an Oriental Girl or a Japanese Girl. I became the Kikokushijo Girl—a returnee, a child who lived abroad because of her father's work. When I went to a high school exclusively for returnees, I stopped being a Kikokushijo Girl, which would have been a redundancy. I should have just become Girl, but I was too *daitan*—written 大胆. Deconstructing the characters reveals much. The first letter simply means *big*. The right side of the second letter is clearly a sun above the horizon—*dawn*. At first glance, the left side looks like the opposite, or *moon*; but it isn't. The two inner strokes were originally angled, not horizontal, a radical form of 肉. 肉 means "flesh, meat, body part." The second letter is the simplified version of gall bladder, courage... or "balls." Combined, the letters "big" and "gall bladder" create a word that translates as "big bravery." In the context of Japanese culture, which depends on conformity, however, the word evokes dis-ease. Its very anatomy leaves no room for the feminine, if the feminine is defined by submission.

Without ever being quite Girl, I graduated from high school in Japan and started college there. I quickly became depressed about my future as Woman. As a female in Japan, I could be a Wife or I could become Office Lady—making coffee for male bosses, trying to find the Husband who would make me Wife. I could fathom myself as neither Office Lady nor Wife. Where would I put my "big balls"? I knew I couldn't continue living there much longer. Then my lungs caught on. I ended up in the hospital, unable to breathe, my oxygen level low enough to require a mask. I left Japan so I wouldn't die.

I ended up in Germany, where I met a Boy. He was Japanese but wore bright yellow pants and spoke loudly—so un-Japanese. I mistook him for the Sun and followed him. Soon, I was Girlfriend. Then I got knocked up. We married, and I found myself back in Japan—this time in rural Mishima with Boy's family. During this time, Boy tried to make me *Yome*: Bride, but *really* Servant. At twenty-two, I said with absolute certainty, "I will not be Yome."

Eventually, we returned to the United States. I refused being Yome, but became Wife. I tended a home for Husband and Baby— soon Babies. I began to lose myself. First, I gave up my bookcases; Husband saw no reason for me to read. Then, I gave up my own taste— Husband deemed it bad. Quickly, I gave up my time, waking up at 3 a.m. to have enough of it, but none to spend on myself. I gave up eating, too. I came to accept that the burden of all the things was for me to bear, and the bad behavior of all the people was for me to bear, and all of me was to be given up, and I became the one with no voice. I became the one clad in a metaphoric kimono, with no one I could confide in about my despair. Somehow, I had managed to become Japanese Wife.

I never became Japanese Woman, however. Japanese Woman would not have left her husband. I left my husband, even though he didn't cheat on me. He did hit me, but that wasn't the reason I left. I left because I was bored—something I know Japanese Woman would never have done.

When I left my marriage with two young children, everything unraveled. I lost friends, family, savings, and profession. I kept only a car and my children. I moved across the country, stopped teaching, and took a job changing bedpans in the emergency department—so I could be home when the children came home. My meal plans involved charging cocktails and fried mozzarella sticks on my credit card at Happy Hour. The kids learned how to do their own laundry and to not ask me for homework help. After they went to bed, I talked on the phone with my college-age boyfriend. Then I stayed up until midnight writing stories about my life as Japanese Wife. To pay for my son's braces, I sold my eggs for five thousand dollars. I was a minority, female, poor, single, raising children alone, breaking taboos, working a menial labor job, and writing at night.

In other words, I was liberated.

Finally, I found my authentic Self. I found my community among the nurses who had my back. I took pride in paying the rent on time. My young boyfriend adored me. I published a story, then another, and another. I once eavesdropped on my daughter telling my son, "We used to be poor, but now we are rich." The truth of this moved me: *We used to be poor, but now we are rich.* For the first time, my identity wasn't determined by the value of others. My life was rich and beautiful, and I loved being Solo Mom with all my heart.

After He Left

Jeanie Tomasko

When the children were small and sleeping,
the night warm and raining,

I would go out to a place under the broken
eaves. Naked, yes. And standing under,

wash my hair with rain and the dark of night.
I could hear cars on the other side

of the duplex. I could smell the sheets
upstairs. I still couldn't touch anything

labeled *future*. Lonely in the rain,
the spirit is beautiful. It can marry

the heart for no one to see. Like I said,
I washed my hair under the broken rain,

and stood there in the night, glistening.

For me, it was the most liberating thing that ever happened to me, having children. If you listen to them, somehow you are able to free yourself from baggage and vanity and all sorts of things and deliver a better self, one that you like. The person that was me, that I liked best, was the one my children seemed to want.

—Toni Morrison

I'd Loved Before, but Never Like This

asha bandele

It's not as though there is anything special my daughter, Nisa, is doing. As I write this, she is leaning back, listening to, I don't know, Future? Drake? But peeking over at her, I still get that same feeling—a rush of life and purpose that true love brings with it.

It wasn't that I hadn't loved before. I had, and each time it felt magical. The Mediterranean husband who gave me a home in Greece when I was 21, only to watch his crippling depression cleave us apart before I turned 25. The second husband, a prisoner, who listened to my poems and made me his wife when I was 28 and a mother when I was 33, deported three months and a day after our daughter was born. Before those men and since, there were other loves—edgy bad boys whose anger I thought was justifiable until they directed it against me rather than the various systems and structures that undid them.

But even with all of them—those romances I thought so epic—
I'd never really known love, the full-bodied freedom of it, until I
became a mother. I had known love contracted by profound sadness
or penetrating rage. Love constrained by barbed wire and armed
guards. Love parsed, love sifted. I had known a measured love, until
I gave birth to my Nisa.

I have this memory: Nisa's not quite two and we're at my
then-boyfriend's house when someone in the crib decides to turn
up, and before you know it, old-school house music is on blast and
the tiny apartment shape-shifts into the legendary Paradise Garage,
circa 1985. Nisa pops up and out of my arms and starts dancing like
there's no world but one of dance, and she is the rhythm and beat,
the rhythm and the beat are her. Her joy, her life: They are infectious
and before I know it, I am shedding my insecurities about how I
dance like a White girl, and I start moving. I swear to God, the boyfriend's Rottweiler does, too, in a dog sort of way. And finally even the
boyfriend—one of those aforementioned bad boys—could no longer
maintain his man scowl, and he's picking me and Nisa up and we are
all hugging and dancing and laughing while the dog runs around us
in excited circles. It was one of the most joyous and free moments in
my life, and it was also the moment I realized why I loved my baby
so much, which wasn't something I ever gave much thought to. I just
loved her; loved her before I even knew her.

But in that hour, in that home, while I cherished her for reasons
too numerous to list, there was one above all: She was free. And in
being her free self, she liberated those around her. She liberated me.
In that room, on that day, and on almost every day after that, with my
Nisa, I am myself, unmasked and free to love as fully and openly as I
know I need to. Love without boundaries. This is no small thing in a
place where Black love of any kind has never been a protected right.

My daughter was the first free person I'd ever known. And for
almost 16 years now, my work has been to protect that freedom with

a love I never knew I was capable of. A-nothing-can-break-it, ain't-no-error-or-misstep-too-great, an all-in kind of love. Which isn't to say she's somehow immune from the terrorism that stalks Black life in general in America or the particular terrorism that makes being a Black girl unsafe. But in this home/life we've created, there's a protected space of freedom that love created. And each morning when I awake I whisper to my Nisa, "Thank you for being my baby, thank you for coming to me." Because for all I am supposed to teach and give her, that girl of mine taught me the greatest lesson of all: how to live, how to love, how to be free.

Contributors

Kim Addonizio ("Gravity" from *The Philosopher's Club* and "All Manner of Obscene Things" from *Bukowski in a Sundress: Confessions from a Writing Life*) is the author of seven poetry collections, two novels, two story collections, and two books on writing poetry, *The Poet's Companion* (with Dorianne Laux) and *Ordinary Genius*. She has received fellowships from the National Endowment for the Arts and Guggenheim Foundation as well as two Pushcart Prizes, and was a National Book Award finalist for her collection *Tell Me*. Her latest books are *Mortal Trash: Poems* and the aforementioned memoir, *Bukowski in a Sundress*. She recently collaborated on a chapbook, *The Night Could Go in Either Direction*, with poet Brittany Perham.

Malaika Albrecht ("How I Came to Me" from *What the Trapeze Artist Trusts*) and her daughters live on Freckles Farm in North Carolina, where they teach yoga and share their lives with a herd of horses, a mini donkey, chickens, ducks, rabbits, cats, and a dog. Solo mom Malaika is the inaugural Heart of Pamlico Poet Laureate, the author of three poetry books, and the founding editor of *Redheaded Stepchild*, an online magazine that accepts only poems that have been rejected elsewhere. As the executive director of Rocking Horse

Ranch, Malaika teaches people with disabilities how to ride and other equine-assisted activities.

Elizabeth Alexander (from *The Light of the World: A Memoir*) is a poet, educator, memoirist, scholar, and arts activist. She is president of the Andrew W. Mellon Foundation and has held distinguished professorships at Smith College, Columbia University, and Yale University. She is a Chancellor of the Academy of American Poets, serves on the Pulitzer Prize Board, and codesigned the Art for Justice Fund, an initiative that addresses the mass incarceration crisis through art and advocacy. *The Light of the World* was a finalist for the Pulitzer Prize and the National Book Critics Circle Award in 2015.

asha bandele ("I'd Loved Before, but Never Like This") is a multi-award-winning and *New York Times* best-selling author of six books and an award-winning journalist. An advocate for human and civil rights and prison abolition, she lives and works in Brooklyn, New York, with her daughter, Nisa, a member of Columbia University's class of 2022.

Akesha Baron ("Origami Wishes") has been published in *Common Ground Review*, *New Millennium Writings*, *Snapdragon Journal*, and an anthology, *Washington 129*, edited by Washington State Poet Laureate Tod Marshall. Her fieldwork with indigenous people in southern Mexico and South Africa led her to appreciate the less solo lives of mothers in a village structure. She has a keen interest in community and hopes to one day open a space where solo moms will always be welcome. Akesha lives in Seattle with her ten-year-old daughter.

Jennifer Baumgardner ("All the Single Ladies" from *F'em! Goo Goo, Gaga, and Some Thoughts on Balls*) is a writer, activist, filmmaker, and lecturer. She is the cofounder of Soapbox, Inc., a speakers' bureau;

the cocreator of Feminist Camp; the editor in chief of the *Women's Review of Books*; and the publisher of Dottir, an independent feminist press. She is the producer of the award-winning documentary *I Had an Abortion* (2005) and the producer and director of *It Was Rape* (2013). Originally from Fargo, North Dakota, Jennifer lives in New York City with her husband, two sons, and two Abyssinian cats.

Jessica Bern ("You Can't 'Undo' This One") is staff editor at *Honey-Suckle* magazine. Her work has appeared on SheKnows and CafeMom, among other publications. She is also a voiceover artist, producer, and video editor. Most importantly, she is surviving parenting a teen with only superficial wounds to the mind and heart. You can see her work at bernthis.com.

VersAnnette Blackman-Bosia ("Why We Stay") is a painter, published poet, speaker, and facilitator. Through her business, Soul Revival Healing Arts, she offers original paintings and products, and teaches workshops. Her first poetry collection, *Butterfly Spirit*, was published in 2015. VersAnnette is passionate about empowering women, eating great food, and traveling the world. A former solo mom, she is ESME's Domestic Violence Resource Guide. She and her family currently reside near Chicago.

Fern Capella ("This is Your Life" from *The Essential Hip Mama: Writing from the Cutting Edge of Parenting*) is an astrologer, a singer/songwriter for the band Star Witness, and a mother residing in the northwest rainforests of the United States. Fern has been published as a poet and writer in various print and online publications, such as *Northwest Edge*, *Hip Mama* magazine, and *Gumball Poetry*.

Ana Castillo ("I Ask the Impossible") was born and raised in Chicago. She is a celebrated and distinguished poet, novelist, short-story writer, essayist, editor, playwright, translator, and independent scholar. Her novel *Sapogonia* was a *New York Times* Notable Book of the Year. She is editor of *La Tolteca*, an arts and literary magazine dedicated to the advancement of a world without borders and censorship. She has held many distinguished teaching posts and, in 1995, won a fellowship from the National Endowment for the Arts for creative writing.

Staceyann Chin ("Coming Out Pregnant!") is a writer, spoken-word artist, and LGBTQ rights and political activist. She starred in and was a cowriter for the Tony-nominated *Russell Simmons Def Poetry Jam* on Broadway and has performed in many one-woman Off-Broadway shows, including her most recent, *MotherStruck!*, which she also wrote. Staceyann's writing has appeared in *Essence*, *Jane*, the *New York Times*, and many other publications, and her poetry has been featured in numerous anthologies—including *Skyscrapers, Taxis, and Tampons*; *Poetry Slam*; and *Butterflies and Bullets*. She is a solo mom who lives with her daughter in New York City.

Courtney Christine ("I'm the Woman Who Hit Your Daughter with My Car") is mother to two smart, brave, and kind little women, who reside with her in Evanston, Illinois. With much trepidation, she began her journey as a solo mom in 2017. Since then, Courtney has rediscovered writing, learned to play the ukulele, and applied for a master's in social work. She's fueled by her daughters' love; they cheer her on every step of the way. Find her blog at medium.com/@courtneychristine.

Teresa Mei Chuc ("The Road") is the poet laureate of Altadena, California (2018–2020); founder and editor-in-chief of Shabda Press; cofounder of The Regenerative Collective, which reintegrates "art, inquiry, and nature into projects that serve poverty-stricken communities and the environment"; and author of three full-length poetry collections—*Red Thread*, *Keeper of the Winds*, and *Invisible Light*—and the recently published anthology *Nuclear Impact: Broken Atoms in Our Hands*. Teresa earned an MFA in creative writing from Goddard College in Plainfield, Vermont, and teaches literature and writing at a public high school in Los Angeles.

Lucille Clifton ("the lost women") wrote numerous poetry collections, children's books, and nonfiction. In 1969, the *New York Times* named her first book of poems, *Good Times*, as one of the best books of the year, and more writing awards followed. She was the poet laureate for the state of Maryland from 1979 to 1985 and the first author to have two poetry collections—*Good Woman: Poems and a Memoir 1969–1980* and *Next: New Poems*—named as finalists for the Pulitzer Prize in the same year (1988). She died in 2010.

Sage Cohen ("How to Pray") is a graduate of Brown University and the Creative Writing Program at New York University. She is the author of the nonfiction books *Fierce on the Page*, *The Productive Writer*, and *Writing the Life Poetic* and the poetry collection *Like the Heart, the World* from Queen of Wands Press. Her poems, essays, and fiction have been published widely, winning a variety of awards and honors. She is the founder of Sage Communications and teaches and lectures nationally at workshops and conferences. She and her son live in Portland, Oregon.

Lisa Fay Coutley ("On Home" from *In the Carnival of Breathing*) is the author of *tether* (forthcoming, 2020); *Errata*, winner of the Crab Orchard Series in Poetry Open Competition Award; and *In the Carnival of Breathing*, winner of the Black River Chapbook Competition. Her recent prose and poetry appears in *AGNI*, *Brevity*, the *Cincinnati Review*, *Narrative*, *Passages North*, *Pleiades*, and the *Los Angeles*

Review. She is an assistant professor of poetry and creative nonfiction in the Writer's Workshop at the University of Nebraska at Omaha.

Meg Day ("What I Will Tell His Daughter, When She Is Old Enough to Ask") is the 2015-2016 recipient of the Amy Lowell Poetry Travelling Scholarship and a 2013 recipient of an NEA Fellowship in Poetry. She is the author of *Last Psalm at Sea Level*, winner of the Barrow Street Poetry Prize and the Publishing Triangle's Audre Lorde Award, and a finalist for the 2016 Kate Tufts Discovery Award from Claremont Graduate University. Meg is an assistant professor of English and creative writing at Franklin & Marshall College and lives in Lancaster, Pennsylvania. To learn more about Meg, visit her website, www.megday.com.

Isa Down ("Tahlequah" and "Myths of Botany and Motherhood") is an artist, writer, and solo mama living in the Rocky Mountains. She is endlessly inspired by nature, which is seen throughout her creative work, and motherhood: "I think I only truly found myself once my son was born, and I was able to proudly name myself a warrior mother. I can be a mom and still create art and words that speak to people." Isa has written for many parenting magazines, and you can follow her creative journey on Instagram at @poppyandgrayco.

Cheryl Dumesnil's ("Yeah, But . . ."; coeditor) books include two collections of poems, *Showtime at the Ministry of Lost Causes* and *In Praise of Falling*; a memoir, *Love Song for Baby X*; and the anthology *Dorothy Parker's Elbow: Tattoos on Writers, Writers on Tattoos*, coedited with Kim Addonizio. When she's not nagging her children to do their homework, she's pitching baseballs to Kid #1 or singing show tunes with Kid #2, while ignoring a sink full of dirty dishes. Her stint as a solo mom ended in 2017, when she married her soul mate, Sarah, aka the Best Stepparent on Earth.

Stacia M. Fleegal ("Teaching My Son to Write: An Abecedarian") is the author of two full-length and three chapbook poetry collections. Her poems have been widely published in literary journals and were nominated for Best of the Net 2017. Her essays have been featured on Salon, Scary Mommy, ESME, and more. Director of the Center for Creative Writing and blogger at Another Writing Mom, Stacia works, writes, solo-moms, plays outside, volunteers, and resists in central Pennsylvania.

Marianne Peel Forman ("Notes to My Autistic Daughter") taught middle and high school English for thirty-two years. Now retired, she does field instructor work at various universities. She is a prize-winning poet whose writing has appeared in *Muddy River Poetry Review*, *Belle Rêve Literary Journal*, *Jelly Bucket*, and many other publications. Marianne is a flute-playing vocalist who is raising four daughters. She shares her life with her partner, Scott. Her poetry was recently published in *Unmasked: Women Write about Sex and Intimacy after 50*, and she has a poetry collection forthcoming from Shadelandhouse Modern Press.

Ylonda Gault ("Why I Don't Grieve for My Daughter at College") is author of the parenting memoir *Child, Please* and an Opinion contributor to the *New York Times*. An award-winning journalist, she specializes in issues related to the Black experience, motherhood, and family. Her essays have been featured in iconic anthologies such as *The Meaning of Michelle*, in which sixteen writers share perspectives on Michelle Obama, and *Queen Bey*, a celebration of the power and creativity of Beyoncé. Ylonda is the editorial director at Planned Parenthood Federation of America and lives in New Jersey with her three awesome children.

Claire Gillespie ("Today, I Am Mostly Crying") is a writer and mom from Ayrshire, Scotland. Before she and her husband created a wonderfully blended family of seven, she was a solo mom to a son and daughter. Her top tip for all solo moms out there? "Self-preserve! Doing the job of two parents can be exhausting. If you make time for yourself, you'll have more time for your kids in all the ways it counts." Her work has been featured in numerous publications, including the *Washington Post*, *Vice*, the *Independent*, Mashable, *Women's Health*, SheKnows.com, and many more.

Susan Goldberg ("Kaboom") is an award-winning writer, editor, blogger, and essayist. Her work has been featured in national publications, including the *New York Times*, the *Globe and Mail*, the *National Post*, *Ms.* magazine, and *Today's Parent*, to name a few. She has written and edited hundreds of articles and has coauthored two books. She is coeditor of the award-winning anthology *And Baby Makes More: Known Donors, Queer Parents, and Our Unexpected Families*. She was born and raised in Toronto and relocated to Thunder Bay, Ontario, in 2004, where she lives with her two sons.

Janlori Goldman ("The Story, for Now") is a poet, teacher, activist, and cofounder of *The Wide Shore: A Journal of Global Women's Poetry*. She has written *Bread from a Stranger's Oven*, her first poetry collection, and *Akhmatova's Egg*, a chapbook; and her poetry has appeared in the *Cortland Review*, *Mead*, *Gwarlingo*, *Connotation Press*, *Calyx*, *Gertrude*, *Mudlark*, the *Sow's Ear*, *Rattle*, and *Contrary*. A queer, single mother, Janlori worked as a civil rights lawyer for nearly twenty years. She is a professor of human rights and public health in New York, and volunteers as a writing mentor at Memorial Sloan Kettering Cancer Center.

Ariel Gore ("Rules for Being Twenty" from *We Were Witches*) is the cofounder, editor, and publisher of the Alternative Press Award–winning magazine *Hip Mama* and the author of several books, including

The Hip Mama Survival Guide; *The Mother Trip*; *The End of Eve*, which chronicles the years she spent caring for her dying mother; and her most recent, *We Were Witches*. She is a graduate of Mills College and the University of California at Berkeley Graduate School of Journalism. Gore has a daughter, Maia, and a son, Maximilian. She currently teaches online at Ariel Gore's School for Wayward Writers.

Janelle Hardy ("Finding My Voice, Feeding My Friends") is an artist, writer, and memoir-writing teacher from Canada's feral northwest. She brings a background in anthropology, dance, Hellerwork Structural Integration, and her searing initiation into adulthood as a solo mother and self-employed creator to her fascination with the ways in which creativity, connection with the body, and reclaiming our life stories can transform our lives. Her solo mom advice? "Seize the empowerment and joy that come from crafting your own path with your child(ren), and don't let the pressure of culture, society, or external judgment shape your life and family identities."

Faleeha Hassan ("My Life as a Refugee") is a poet, teacher, editor, writer, and playwright born in Najaf, Iraq, in 1967, who now lives in the United States. She is the first woman to publish poetry for children in Iraq. Faleeha earned her master's degree in Arabic literature and has published twenty books. Her poems have been translated into many languages, including English, Turkmen, French, Italian, German, Kurdish, Spanish, Korean, Greek, and Albanian. She has received many awards in Iraq and throughout the Middle East for her poetry and short stories.

Kristie Robin Johnson ("Evening Guilt") is an educator, essayist, and poet from Augusta, Georgia. She is a graduate of the MFA Creative Writing program at Georgia College and State University. Kristie's writing has been nominated for a Pushcart Prize and Association of

Writers & Writing Programs honors, and has received other awards and recognition. Her work has appeared or is forthcoming in *Rigorous*, *Split Lip* magazine, ESME, *Under the Gum Tree*, *Lunch Ticket*, *riverSedge*, and other journals and publications. She resides in Grovetown, Georgia, with her two sons.

Muriel Johnson ("Personals" from *The Essential Hip Mama: Writings from the Cutting Edge of Parenting*) grew up in Salisbury, Maryland, in an environment where language was celebrated. A born storyteller, she has performed at pre-K and elementary schools, churches, museums, colleges, festivals, and countless other venues from rural communities in the United States to the townships of Cape Town, South Africa. Muriel has been a featured storyteller as well as an emcee at the renowned Sierra Storytelling Festival in California. Muriel lives in the San Francisco Bay Area, is the mother of three children, and has been an early childhood educator for more than twenty years.

Mary Karr ("The Nervous Hospital" from *Lit*) is the critically acclaimed author of three best-selling memoirs—*The Liars' Club*, *Cherry*, and *Lit*. A distinguished poet, she has written five poetry collections, including her most recent, *Tropic of Squalor*, published in 2018. Mary is the Peck Professor of Literature at Syracuse University.

Lennlee Keep ("Dad Day: Death Is a Holiday") is a nonfiction writer, filmmaker, storyteller, and mother of a teenaged boy named Dash. Her writing has appeared in the Rumpus and the *Southeast Review*, and her films have been shown on PBS, A&E, and the BBC. The ex-wife of a dead guy, she talks about grief more than most people are comfortable with. She is working on a memoir about addiction, grief, and a heart so broken it required surgery. That said, she is much funnier than the preceding two sentences might lead you to believe.

Margot Kessler ("The Godfather") is a writer, occasionally witty commentator, and often disorganized solo mother of two young women. She has several regrets about her life choices, but having children is not one of them. She is still astonished she has managed to muddle through thus far.

Sharisse Kimbro ("For My Sisters") is a writer, mother, and stepmother who resides in the Chicago area. She has written extensively on empowering women, recovery from divorce, and managing single parenthood for a variety of outlets, including ESME, Divorced Moms, and For Harriet. Her debut novel, *Beyond the Broken*, published in 2013, is a powerful story about what happens when the life you planned for isn't the life you end up with. She is currently working on her second novel.

Sarah Kowalski ("Teacher and Teammate") is ESME's Solo Mom by Choice Resource Guide, a somatic coach, Feldenkrais practitioner, and qigong teacher, specializing in the mind/body connection. As the founder of Motherhood Reimagined, she coaches women through their emotions and fears so that solo motherhood, egg donation, adoption, or other means can become an option to consider. She helps women redefine what it means to be a mother so they can cultivate the love, courage, and tenacity it takes to conceive and raise a child by unconventional means.

Jacob Kronenberg ("It's Really Not a Big Deal") was raised in Evanston, Illinois, by not one, but two wonderful solo moms. He's currently pursuing his PhD in chemical engineering at New York University, but when he's not in the lab, he enjoys cooking, reading, and exploring the city he calls home.

Keetje Kuipers ("Prayer") is the author of three poetry collections: *Beautiful in the Mouth*, winner of the A. Poulin, Jr. Poetry Prize; *The*

314 | We Got This

Keys to the Jail; and, most recently, *All Its Charms*. Her poems, essays, and short stories have appeared in *Best American Poetry*, *Narrative*, *American Poetry Review*, *Orion*, *Prairie Schooner*, *The Writer's Almanac*, and the Academy of American Poets' Poem-a-Day series. Keetje lives with her wife and daughter on an island in the Salish Sea, where she is a faculty member at Seattle's Hugo House and senior editor at *Poetry Northwest*.

Kathleen Laccinole ("Raising a Boy without a Man"), ESME's Dating Resource Guide, has penned numerous films and parenting books but is best known for producing the highly lauded Greta, age 20, and William, age 16.

Anne Lamott ("September 17" from *Operating Instructions: A Journal of My Son's First Year*) is the author of numerous *New York Times* best sellers, including *Some Assembly Required*, *Bird by Bird*, and *Operating Instructions* (which chronicles her single mom journey during her son's first year of life), to name a few. She is a past recipient of a Guggenheim Fellowship and an inductee to the California Hall of Fame. Her most recent essay collection, *Almost Everything: Notes on Hope*, was published in 2018.

Dorianne Laux ("Return") is the author of numerous poetry collections, including *What We Carry*, a finalist for the National Book Critics Circle Award; *Facts about the Moon*, recipient of the Oregon Book Award and short-listed for the Lenore Marshall Poetry Prize; and *The Book of Men*, recipient of the Paterson Prize. Dorianne teaches poetry in the Program in Creative Writing at North Carolina State University and is a founding faculty member of Pacific University's Low Residency MFA Program. Her most recent collection, *Only as the Day Is Long: New and Selected*, was published earlier this year.

Shannon Lell ("Divorce Cliché") is a writer and yoga and mountain-bike enthusiast who lives in Seattle with her two children. Her best parenting tip? "Have fun with your children as much as possible," and, "above all else, promote reading and the importance of art" because, she says, they both "teach empathy." Her writing has been published in the *Washington Post*, Longreads, the Rumpus, Scary Mommy, and more. She is currently writing a memoir about her political, sexual, and spiritual awakening in midlife.

Marika Lindholm ("Butterfly and Sunshine"; coeditor) founded the social platform Empowering Solo Moms Everywhere (ESME) to ignite a social movement of solo moms. A trained sociologist, she taught courses on inequality, diversity, and gender at Northwestern University for over a decade. Marika has published scholarly articles; been a regular contributor to *Psychology Today*, *Working Mother*, mindbodygreen, and Talkspace; and published essays and fiction in the *Daily News*, *Elephant Journal*, the *Hill*, *Ms.*, *Silent Voices*, and the *Southern Indiana Review*.

P. Charlotte Lindsay ("I Don't Want Your Husband") is a middle-aged single mom and expert in the world of online dating. Following her divorce, she went on 300 dates (garnered online) in three years. She now uses her experience to guide others who are reentering the dating pool in the age of technology on how to meet guys, get laid, and maybe even find love. She is a real person, though her name has been changed to protect the innocent, namely her children and parents. You can follow her on Facebook at @pcharlottelindsaytlc, on Twitter at @pcharlottetlc, and on Instagram at @pcharlottelindsay.

Terri Linton ("When One Door Closes, Another One Opens") holds a juris doctor degree from Rutgers School of Law–Newark and is pursuing a master's degree in creative nonfiction writing from Sarah

Lawrence College. A professor of writing and criminal justice at New York colleges, Terri is also a freelance writer and host of the podcast *She Roads with Terri Linton*. Terri's writing appears on her blog, *She Is Terri Linton*; ESME; *Ninth Letter*; HuffPost; Motherly; and Mamamia. She lives in New York with her son and is working on a memoir.

Audre Lorde ("Now That I Am Forever with Child") was a poet, essayist, novelist, mother, teacher, feminist, civil rights activist, and librarian. In the 1980s, she received the Gay Caucus Book of the Year Award for *The Cancer Journals*, which chronicles her battles with cancer, and a National Book Award for *A Burst of Light*. She cofounded Kitchen Table: Women of Color Press, the first US publisher for women of color. She was an English professor at John Jay College of Criminal Justice, and from 1991 to 1992, she was the poet laureate of New York. She died in 1992.

Hilary Melton ("In a Quiet Moment") is the founder and executive director of Pathways Vermont, an agency that works to end chronic homelessness in communities across the state of Vermont by providing housing and innovative mental health services. She received her MFA from Vermont College of Fine Arts. Her work has appeared in the *New York Quarterly*, *Ellipsis*, *Rattle*, *Slipstream*, and the *Sow's Ear Poetry Review*, among others.

Cate Morrissey ("My Birth, My Way"), not the author's real name, is a solo mom and freelance writer. Her writing has appeared in numerous online and print publications. She is a regular contributor to ESME, where she writes about the many facets of being a single mom.

Abby Murray ("How to Comfort a Small Child") has an MFA from Pacific University and a PhD from Binghamton University. She is the editor of *Collateral*, a journal publishing work concerned with the impact of violent conflict and military service beyond the combat zone. Her most recent chapbook, *How to Be Married after Iraq*, was published in 2018, and her recent poems can be found in *Rattle: Poets Respond*, *New Ohio Review*, and *Prairie Schooner*. Abby was raised with five sisters by a solo mom.

Lee Nash ("They Give Awards for That") lives in France and has been a single mother to her two children since 2008. Her poems have appeared in many print and online journals, and her first poetry chapbook, *Ash Keys*, was published in 2017. The following year, she received a Bath Flash Fiction Award. Her solo mom tip is to hold on to your dignity, however undignified you may feel, whatever you may have lost, and however unfair your situation; your self-respect is not for the taking. Read more about Lee on her website, leenashpoetry.com.

Sarah Netter ("Life after the NICU"), ESME's Adoption Resource Guide, is a single mother by choice to a fabulous little boy, one neurotic Italian Greyhound, and two Spanish Galgo puppies. She is a full-time journalist whose work has appeared in the *New York Times*, the *Washington Post*, and ABC News.

January Gill O'Neil ("The Rookie," "How to Love," and "Sunday") was born in Norfolk, Virginia, and received a BA from Old Dominion University and an MFA from New York University. She is the author of *Misery Islands* (winner of a 2015 Paterson Award for Literary Excellence) and *Underlife*. She has received fellowships from Cave Canem and the Barbara Deming Memorial Fund. The executive director of the Massachusetts Poetry Festival, January also serves on the Association of Writers and Writing Programs' board of directors and teaches at Salem State University. She lives in Beverly, Massachusetts.

Deborah Oster Pannell ("When Black Lives Matter More Than You Ever Imagined") is a freelance writer, editor, and curator who collaborates with other writers, artists, and creative entrepreneurs to develop and promote new projects. After her husband died, she became a solo mom, which she describes as "the most challenging yet rewarding experience of my life." She writes about love, loss, parenting, race, social justice, spirituality, and sexuality, with an eye toward building community and contributing to a more compassionate and humane society.

Georgia Pearle ("This Lesson I Know My Boy Already Knows") is an alumna of Smith College and holds an MFA in poetry from Lesley University. Her poems have appeared in *Kenyon Review Online*, *Crab Creek Review*, and *Women's Studies Quarterly*, among others. The digital editor for *Gulf Coast: A Journal for Literature and Fine Arts* from 2016–2018, she recently received her PhD in creative writing and literature from the University of Houston. She is the 2018 recipient of the Inprint Marion Barthelme Prize in Creative Writing. She lives in Houston with her two children.

Evie Peck ("Size Queen") is an actor, writer, and producer living in Los Angeles. As a solo mom by choice, she says her solo parenting hack is for all human beings: "Do not be fooled by the curated lives you see on social media or in magazines or even right next door.... Focus on your own reality without comparison." Evie cowrote and performed in a hit play about bad dates called *I Made Out with Him Anyway*. She writes about being a solo mom on her blog, www.momsolo.com.

Amy Poehler ("My Books on Divorce" from *Yes Please*) is a writer, comedian, and actress, best known as a cast member on *Saturday Night Live* and for her role as Leslie Knope on the NBC sitcom *Parks and Recreation*. The mother of two sons, Amy is a fierce advocate for children and women: she's the cofounder of Smart Girls, a web series dedicated to helping young people cultivate their authentic selves, and is Ambassador of Arts for the Worldwide Orphans Foundation, with which she has been involved for many years. Her debut memoir, *Yes Please*, was published in 2014.

Nisa Rashid ("I Was the Different One") is a graduate of the Brooklyn Friends School in New York City and currently attends Columbia University. Her first published work, "The Drug Education Teens Really Need," appeared in HuffPost when she was fifteen.

Adrienne Rich ("XIII" from "Twenty-One Love Poems") published nonfiction as well as numerous poetry collections, including *Tonight No Poetry Will Serve: Poems 2007–2010*; *The School Among the Ruins: Poems 2000–2004*, which won the Book Critics Circle Award; *Collected Early Poems: 1950–1970*; *An Atlas of the Difficult World: Poems 1988–1991*, a finalist for the National Book Award (an award she won in 1974 for *Diving into the Wreck*); and *The Dream of a Common Language*. In 1997, she received the Academy of American Poets' Wallace Stevens Award for outstanding and proven mastery in the art of poetry. She died in 2012.

Angela Ricketts ("Grey Street") is the author of the memoir *No Man's War: Irreverent Confessions of an Infantry Wife*, in which "Grey Street" appears, and is ESME's Military Resource Guide. Daughter and wife of career infantrymen, she has a master's degree in social psychology. You can follow her on Twitter at @angricketts and on Facebook at @AngMacRicketts.

Amy Rivers ("We Are Loved") grew up in southern New Mexico and currently resides in Colorado with her family. Her graduate work focused on politics, psychology, and forensic criminology, topics she loves to incorporate into her personal essays and novels. Amy has been published in *Chicken Soup for the Soul: Inspiration for Nurses*, *Novelty Bride* magazine, and Splice Today, as well as several fiction anthologies. She is the author of two novels, *Wallflower Blooming* and *Best Laid Plans & Other Disasters*. Her third novel, *All the Broken People*, was published earlier this year.

Robin Rogers ("When He Died") is on the faculty of the sociology department at Queens College, City University of New York, where she serves as the director of Honors in the Social Sciences. Her sordid academic past includes working as a Congressional Fellow on Capitol Hill, receiving her PhD from the University of Pennsylvania, doing postdoctoral work at Yale University, teaching as a visiting professor at Princeton University, writing a book on welfare reform, and assorted other scholarly detritus. She has two sons and is currently researching Generation X women.

Domenica Ruta ("You Were Born to Be Loved"; coeditor) is the author of the *New York Times* bestseller *With or Without You*, a memoir about growing up with a heroin-addicted solo mom. Her short fiction has appeared in *Epoch*, *Indiana Review*, and the *Boston Review*. Her most recent book, *Last Day*, a novel, was written in a postpartum fugue state as a new solo mom to her son. She lives in New York City. You can follow her on Twitter at @DomenicaMary and on Instagram at @domenicaruta.

Rachel Sarah ("How My Daughter Taught Me to Trust Again") is the author of *Single Mom Seeking*, which was optioned for television by 20th Century Fox. In 2012, she and her husband, Chris, welcomed a second daughter. You can find her online at www.rachel sarah.com, on Twitter at @Rachel__Sarah, and on Instagram at @rachel_sarah_writes.

Jaimie Seaton ("What Remains") has been a freelance journalist for more than twenty years. She is the divorced mother of two awesome teenagers and often writes about parenting, dating, and relationships. Her work has appeared in numerous publications worldwide, including the *Guardian*, the Establishment, *Glamour*, and the *Washington Post*. Follow her on Twitter at @JaimieSeaton.

Nancy Sharp ("The Sky Is Everywhere," from her award-winning memoir, *Both Sides Now: A True Story of Love, Loss, and Bold Living*) is an author, keynote speaker, and storyteller who frequently speaks publicly about loss, transformation, and bold living. She lives in Denver with her second husband, her twins, and her two stepsons. You can find her on Twitter at @boldlivingnow and on Facebook at @NancySharpVividLiving.

Katherine Shonk (coeditor) is the author of the short-story collection *The Red Passport* and the novel *Happy Now?* Her writing has appeared in *Best American Short Stories*, *Tin House*, and elsewhere. An editor for ESME and Harvard University, Katherine lives with her family in Evanston, Illinois, where she is working on a novel about motherhood and immigration.

Robin Silbergleid ("An Open Letter to Our Sperm Donor" and "Crying It Out") is the author of *The Baby Book*, a collection of poems, and the memoir *Texas Girl*, as well as coeditor of *Reading and Writing Experimental Texts: Critical Innovations*. Currently, she teaches at Michigan State University, where she directs the Creative Writing Program. Since 2014, she has led writing workshops on reproductive loss with the international art, oral history, and portraiture project *The ART of Infertility*. She is a single mother by choice of two and lives with her family in East Lansing, Michigan.

Anne Spollen ("Heroin, Rain") is mom to three young adult children. She is a professor of English and composition for Ocean County College in New Jersey and teaches in the Adult Literacy Program for the City University of New York Research Foundation. She is the author of two novels and has been widely published as a poet, essayist, and fiction writer. She is completing a multigenre book about the impact addiction has had on her family. She is also working on a novel set in New York City during the 1960s that explores the theme of learned racism.

Melissa Stephenson ("When a Car Wreck Collides with Picking Up the Kids") has written for publications including *Lit Hub*, the *Washington Post*, *ZYZZYVA*, Waxwing, and *Fourth Genre*. Her memoir, *Driven*, was published last year. She lives in Missoula, Montana, with her two kids.

Ruth Stone ("Then") published thirteen books of poetry, including *What Love Comes To: New and Selected Poems*, a finalist for the Pulitzer Prize in 2009; *In the Next Galaxy*, which received the 2002 National Book Award; and *Ordinary Words*, which received the National Book Critics Circle Award. After her second husband died, she continued raising their three daughters while teaching English and creative writing at several universities, earning tenure at the State University of New York at Binghamton at age seventy-seven. She served as the state poet of Vermont from 2007 until close to her death in 2011.

Kelly Sundberg ("It Will Look Like a Sunset") is the author of the memoir *Goodbye, Sweet Girl: A Story of Domestic Violence and Survival*, released by HarperCollins in 2018. Her essays have appeared in or are forthcoming from *Alaska Quarterly Review*, *Guernica*, *Gulf Coast*, *Denver Quarterly*, and other literary journals. She has been the recipient of grants and fellowships from A Room of Her Own Foundation, Dickinson House, Vermont Studio Center, and the National Endowment for the Arts. She has a PhD in creative nonfiction from Ohio University, where she is currently a visiting assistant professor.

Jeanie Tomasko ("After He Left") is the author of several poetry chapbooks, including *The Collect of the Day*; *Dove Tail*; *Violet Hours*; *Small Towns along the Coast*; *(Prologue)*, winner of the 2013 Concrete Wolf Editor's Choice award; and her most recent, *dear little fist*. She can be found walking her grand-dog in Middleton, Wisconsin, or at home with her husband, Steve. She endeavors to always have a bottomless honey jar, garlic from the garden, and bees in the front yard hyssop. Jeanie is a registered nurse and works in home health. See more of her writing and artwork at www.jeanietomasko.com.

Jen Waite (excerpt from *A Beautiful, Terrible Thing: A Memoir of Marriage and Betrayal*) is a single mom who lives with her young daughter in Maine. Her writing has appeared in Scary Mommy, Upworthy, Romper, and HuffPost. She is moving toward becoming a licensed therapist, specializing in recovery from trauma, and has an upcoming memoir on psychopathy and thriving after trauma. Check out her blog, www.jenwaite.com.

Rachel Jamison Webster ("Cicadas") directs the creative writing program at Northwestern University, where she also teaches poetry and creative nonfiction, and designs curricula in representation, diversity, and literary ethics. She is the author of *September: Poems*; *The Endless Unbegun*; *Mary is a River*; and a forthcoming memoir. She has published two chapbooks, *Hazel and the Mirror* and *The Blue Grotto*, and her poems, stories, and essays appear in dozens of anthologies and journals, including *Poetry, Tin House, Narrative,* the *Southern Review,* and the *Paris Review.* She lives with her daughter, Adele, in Evanston, Illinois.

Mika Yamamoto ("Deconstructing Kanji") is a writer and ESME's Public Assistance Resource Guide. Her work can be found in *Noon, Nelle,* Hawai'i Pacific Review, the Rumpus, and other publications.

Permissions and Acknowledgments

CHAPTER ONE: THE KIDS ARE ALRIGHT

"The Road," by Teresa Mei Chuc, has been reprinted with permission from the author.

From *The Light of the World: A Memoir*, by Elizabeth Alexander. Copyright © 2015 by Elizabeth Alexander. Used by permission of Grand Central Publishing.

The original version of "When One Door Closes, Another One Opens," by Terri Linton, was published on ESME.com.

"Notes to My Autistic Daughter," by Marianne Peel Forman, was published on ESME.com

"I Was the Different One," by Nisa Rashid, copyright © 2017 by Nisa Rashid, published in *He Never Came Home: Interviews, Stories, and*

CHAPTER TWO: LEAN ON ME

CHAPTER THREE: A DAY IN THE LIFE
"When a Car Wreck Collides with Picking Up the Kids," by Melissa Stephenson, was published on ESME.com.

"How to Comfort a Small Child," by Abby Murray, has been reprinted with permission from the author.

Ariel Gore, "Rules for Being Twenty," from *We Were Witches*. Copyright © 2017 by Ariel Gore. Reprinted with the permission of the Permissions Company, Inc., on behalf of the Feminist Press, www.feministpress.org. All rights reserved.

"Evening Guilt," by Kristie Robin Johnson, was published on ESME.com.

"Faleeha Hassan: My Life as a Refugee," by Faleeha Hassan, translated by William M. Hutchins, appeared in the online literary magazine *Empty Mirror* and has been reprinted with permission from the author.

"The Rookie," by January Gill O'Neil. Reproduced from *Prairie Schooner* 89.4 (Winter 2015) by permission of the University of Nebraska Press. Copyright © 2015 by the University of Nebraska Press.

"This Is Your Life," by Fern Capella, from pages 5–8 of *The Essential Hip Mama: Writing from the Cutting Edge of Parenting*, has been reprinted with permission from the author.

"Crying It Out," by Robin Silbergleid, was published on ESME.com.

"They Give Awards for That," by Lee Nash, was published on ESME.com.

CHAPTER FOUR: GOOD MORNING HEARTACHE

"Why We Stay," by VersAnnette Blackman-Bosia, was published on ESME.com.

"When He Died," by Robin Rogers, was published on ESME.com.

Quote from Terri Linton's Sister Note for ESME ("A Welcome Note from Your ESME Incarceration Resource Guide, Terri Linton") has been reprinted with permission from the author.

From *The Light of the World: A Memoir*, by Elizabeth Alexander. Copyright © 2015 by Elizabeth Alexander. Used by permission of Grand Central Publishing.

"Family in 3/4 Time" © 2015 by Elizabeth Alexander, is used with the permission of Elizabeth Alexander.

"Then," from *Ordinary Words* © 1999 by Ruth Stone. Published by Wesleyan University Press (via Paris Press) and reprinted with permission.

The original version of "When Black Lives Matter More Than You Ever Imagined," by Deborah Oster Pannell, was published on ESME.com.

"In a Quiet Moment," by Hilary Melton, appeared in the Fall 2013 issue of *Rattle* (#41) and has been reprinted with permission from the author.

"On Home," by Lisa Fay Coutley, appeared in her poetry collection *In the Carnival of Breathing*, published in 2011 by Black Lawrence Press and reprinted here with permission from Black Lawrence Press and Southern Illinois University Press.

CHAPTER FIVE: A CHANGE IS GONNA COME

CHAPTER SIX: ISN'T IT ROMANTIC?

CHAPTER SEVEN: HERE COMES THE SUN

Quote by Toni Morrison, taken from Bill Moyers's March 1990 interview titled "Toni Morrison on Love and Writing (Part 1)," has been reprinted with permission from the author and Judy Doctoroff.

"I'd Loved Before, but Never Like This," by asha bandele. Copyright © 2016 by asha bandele. Published by *Ebony* on February 10, 2016 (www.ebony.com/life/love-black-motherhood/), and reprinted with permission from the author.

Acknowledgments

From start to finish, *We Got This: Solo Mom Stories of Grit, Heart, and Humor* has been a labor of love. The four of us connected over the idea that solo moms deserved a book just for them. We knew it would be a lot of work, and we knew it would be worth it, but we didn't know that our collaboration would bring so much joy. Thus, we begin by acknowledging the mutual affection, respect, and love that's thrived through all the Google Hangouts, emails, and texts flying between San Francisco, Chicago, New York City, and the Hudson Valley. We kept at this project while working other jobs and parenting nine children among us, all the while growing closer as collaborators and friends.

Passion propelled us, but without some key allies, our vision would have been impossible to realize. Our first shout-out goes to the indefatigable Heidi Kronenberg, ESME.com's director of operations and our number-one cheerleader, who connected us with solo mom writers and helped us stay organized as we read through countless submissions. Deven Connelly, ESME's content manager, was the keeper of the Google Drive document and ringleader of our weekly Hangouts. His good humor and heart got us through long sessions as we hammered out the best placement for a poem or quote and then changed our mind 47 times. Philip Graham validated and invigorated our desire to showcase great writing by solo moms when he invited us to assemble a special feature in *Ninth Letter*, titled "Solo Mom Sessions." We are also grateful to Melissa Snyder, who patiently compiled and proofread 70-plus bios and our numerous permission lines. The ever-energetic Barrett Briske relentlessly reached out to authors, publishers, and agents to secure rights to the work of many talented solo moms. It really does take a village, and in our case, we benefited from a community of solo moms who shared their heartache, humor, and experiences. Our incredible solo mom contributors, representing the many millions of solo moms across the world, inspired and humbled us, and we are honored to share their stories.

Our final thank you must go to our children, who make us want to do better and be better as parents, role models, and change makers. Thank you to Domenica's little Zeke, Katie's Lillian, Cheryl's Brennan and Kian, and Ella, Jonas, Wini, Beck, and Sofia—Marika's crew—for adding flavor and heart to all that we do. Finally, a grateful woof to our mascot, Hugo the French bulldog, who understands that giving and getting love is the essence of life.

SELECTED TITLES FROM SHE WRITES PRESS

She Writes Press is an independent publishing company founded to serve women writers everywhere. Visit us at www.shewritespress.com.

Make a Wish for Me: A Mother's Memoir by LeeAndra Chergey. $16.95, 978-1-63152-828-6. A life-changing diagnosis teaches a family that where there is love, there is hope—and that being "normal" is not nearly as important as providing your child with a life full of joy, love, and acceptance.

Peanut Butter and Naan: Stories of an American Mother in the Far East by Jennifer Hillman-Magnuson. $16.95, 978-1-63152-911-5. The hilarious tale of what happened when Jennifer Hillman-Magnuson moved her family of seven from Nashville to India in an effort to shake things up—and got more than she bargained for.

The Buddha at My Table: How I Found Peace in Betrayal and Divorce by Tammy Letherer. $16.95, 978-1-63152-425-7. On a Tuesday night, just before Christmas, after he had put their three children in bed, Tammy Letherer's husband shattered her world and destroyed every assumption she'd ever made about love, friendship, and faithfulness. In the aftermath of this betrayal, however, she finds unexpected blessings—and, ultimately, the path to freedom.

Stepmother: A Memoir by Marianne Lile. $16.95, 978-1-63152-089-1. Lile describes the complexities of the stepmom position, in a family and in the community, and shares her experience wearing a tag that is often misunderstood and weighed down by the numerous myths in society.

Science of Parenthood: Thoroughly Unscientific Explanations for Utterly Baffling Parenting Situations by Norine Dworkin-McDaniel and Jessica Ziegler. $19.95, 978-1-63152-947-4. A satirical take on the early years of parenting that uses faux math, snarky science, and irreverent cartoons to offer hilarious hypotheses for parenting's most perplexing mysteries.

Times They Were A-Changing: Women Remember the '60s & '70s edited by Kate Farrell, Amber Lea Starfire, and Linda Joy Myers. $16.95, 978-1-938314-04-9. Forty-eight powerful stories and poems detailing the breakthrough moments experienced by women during the '60s and '70s.